TRILATERALS OVER WASHINGTON II

TRILATERALS OVER WASHINGTON II

ANTONY C. SUTTON
PATRICK M. WOOD

PUBLISHED BY
THE AUGUST CORPORATION

THE AUGUST CORPORATION
P.O. BOX 582
SCOTTSDALE, ARIZONA 85251

1st Printing — March 1981

Library of Congress Catalog Card Number 78-78277
International Standard Book Number 0-933482-02-7

Published in the United States by

THE AUGUST CORPORATION

Communicating through print and broadcast media to people around the world, intelligence that will increase personal awareness of political, economic, social and spiritual trends in order to encourage specific prayer and motivate effective action.

Merchants have no country. The mere spot they stand on does not constitute so strong an attachment as that from which they draw their gains.

Thomas Jefferson
Letter to Horatio G. Spafford
[March 17, 1814]

PREFACE

"We have councils of Vocations, Councils of Eugenics, every possible kind of Council, including a World Council — and if these do not as yet hold total power over us, is it from lack of intention?

"Some might think — though I don't — that nine years ago there was some excuse for men not to see the direction in which the world was going. Today, the evidence is so blatant that no excuse can be claimed by anyone any longer. Those who refuse to see it now are neither blind nor innocent."

Author's Foreward, *Anthem*
Ayn Rand, 1946

In the two years since Volume I of *Trilaterals Over Washington*, the "sleeping giant" has barely awakened to yawn before going back to sleep. While then hardly anybody in the U.S. had heard of the Trilateral Commission, now somewhere around 10 per cent are aware of its existence.

In spite of this increased awareness, as this Volume II will demonstrate, little has been done to curtail or forestall the rise of Trilateralism.

The authors' view of Trilateralism and of many Trilateral

i

Commission members has "mellowed" considerably since Volume I was written. More research, many personal contacts with members of the Commission and extensive travel have all contributed to this change.

A certain percentage of members are indeed sincere in their quest for Trilateralism, albeit sincerely wrong (in the authors' estimation). Others are not so innocent, and are quietly deceptive and misleading about their motives in creating a New Economic World Order.

We find that the Trilateral Commission, per se, is not attempting to create a world government — *that* is nonchalantly left to other forums and organizations, in which one finds many individual Trilateral Commissioners, but not the Trilateral Commission itself.

The Commission is dedicated to creating a *New Economic World Order* as opposed to a Political World Order. They cannot be directly or fairly criticized for the latter. Indirectly, of course, there are many close connections.

Neither is the Trilateral Commission a "conspiracy." The authors have been able to secure information about the Commission without undue hardship — this book proves it. The authors do not pass judgement on the legality of any specific act of this alleged "conspiracy"; that should be left for a court or a Congressional investigation.

In short, in order to properly expose the details and plans of Trilateralism it is not necessary or desirable to argue over what one *doesn't* know. The Trilateral elite is operating in full daylight, but few are willing to say "Halt!"

Meanwhile, America continues to live in a state of fantasy, unable to discern reality amidst a myriad of surrealistic stimuli. America continues to be literally brainwashed by the electronic media, but not that it was all intended that way — to a large extent, Americans are getting exactly what they asked for!

Is America calming down to the serious business of saving the world from itself by embracing atheistic Humanism? Hardly. Americans spend more than $2.3 billion per year on tranquilizers. Of the $3.34 billion per year on the thirteen most popular medications sold, eighteen percent ($600 million) is for the tranquilizer *Valium*. $1.2 billion (another 36 per cent) goes for ulcer and high blood pressure medicine.

Psychiatrists and psychologists are booked solid and different types of therapy cults are springing up all over. Families are being dissolved at an unprecedented rate, suicides are up and the still rising crime rate cannot be slowed.

Where is the world really headed? If you don't at least have an opinion after reading this book, you are in serious trouble.

How can you protect yourself? Consider this 3,000 year old masterpiece of wisdom:

> *"Do not say, 'why is it that the former days were better than these?' For it is not from wisdom that you ask about this. Wisdom along with an inheritance is good and an advantage to those who see the sun. For wisdom is protection just as money is protection. But the advantage is that wisdom preserves the lives of its possessors. Consider the work of God, for who is able to straighten what He has bent? In the day of adversity consider — God has made the one as well as the other so that man may not discover anything that will be after him."*

King Solomon
Ecclesiastes Ch. 7, v. 10 - 14

FOOTNOTES PREFACE

1. Ayn Rand, *Anthem,* p. 12.
2. *Ecclesiastes,* Chapter 7, verses 10-14, New American Standard Bible.

CONTENTS

CHAPTER ONE

INTRODUCTION

Trilaterals Over Washington-Volume II, is the continuation from Volume I of the saga of the Trilateral elite. The areas of focus in Volume II are essentially different: we delve into the philosophy of "Globalism," new major economic developments, foreign policy and European Trilateralism.

One of the outstanding characteristics of the Trilateral **Carter** Administration was its pragmatic use of human rights for international elitist objectives. While Trilateral writing on human rights is scant, the Administration proclaimed to the world that it had deep concern for human rights around the world and that this concern was a basic premise of U.S. policy.

We have described in some detail how the Trilateral position on human rights is two-faced. On the one hand we present the plight of Russian Christians seeking refuge in the American Embassy in Moscow and attempts to have them returned to the dictatorship from which they were fleeing: their return will mean lengthy imprisonment as payment for their efforts to obtain human rights. On the other hand we point out the double standard with events in South Africa and Communist Hungary. Specific examples of **Henry Kissinger's** use of human rights as a so-called "gambling chip" are cited.

We have clearly set forth in Chapter Two the operating "philosophy" of Trilateralism, that is, *Humanism*. According to the Humanist Manifesto[1] (the "constitution" of Humanism), "No deity will save us: we must save ourselves." Pointedly atheistic, Humanism-Trilateralism is spewing out "saviors" who are implementing their own self-righteous programs while thinking they are doing us a favor by preparing a brighter future for mankind. But is it so innocent? You may not think so after seeing how Humanism and Communism both were spawned from the same group in the early 1900's. That the Trilaterals and Marxist countries can and do work together comfortably is no surprise.

Another area of concern to many Americans is the movement in schools across the country to create "global citizens" out of America's youth, paving the way for easy and painless implementation of "interdependence." This re-education of America is being funded by the same foundations that fund the Trilateral Commission. This is brought out in Chapter Three.

Chapters Four and Five take a look at the manner in which Trilateralism transcends political systems, particularly in the context of the historically erroneous theme of Capitalism versus Marxism. The broadly held idea that Capitalists are the enemies of Marxists misses the mark. The Trilateral Commission is continuing and indeed emphasizing a long-run cooperation between a segment of capitalist elitists and the emerging Marxist world. We cite, for example, former Secretary of State **Cyrus Vance,** a member of the law firm, Simpson, Thacher and Bartlett; this is the same law firm that in October 1918 prevailed upon Woodrow Wilson to recognize the then-new Soviet regime in Russia.

Chapter Five also points out some history behind groups that have dominated foreign policy since at least 1921 — the latest of which is the Trilateral Commission. Historically, the most important of these is the Council on Foreign Relations (CFR) founded in 1920. But we should not ignore the Foreign Policy Association, the Atlantic Council and the Rockefeller Commission on Critical Choices for Americans. We show the extraordinary interlock between these organizations; for example, more than 24 percent of Trilaterals are also CFR members.

In Chapter Six we compare two examples of Trilateral foreign policy and human rights. First the case of Communist China and second the case of the Panama Canal Treaty. The Trilateral agreements with Communist China were concluded in the face of the murder of over one hundred million Chinese by the Communist regime.[2]

While China has possibly the worst record of genocide in history, it was overlooked for a reason similar to that in the early 1920's when Wall Street and the European financial elite built up the USSR — *profit.*

Normalization of relations with China will dramatically change the economic structure of the world within a few short years as the Trilateral process exploits slave labor in China at the expense of free labor forces in the US and abroad.

The Panama Canal debacle is another case of hypocrisy and double standards. That the Panama Canal had been bought and fully paid for many years ago by the U.S. was not discussed at the Congressional hearings that led to the giving away of the Canal. Would Texans squawk if the administration unilaterally gave Texas — undisputed U.S. territory — back to Mexico?

Understatement aside, we found that of the 30 or so banks that had made rather shaky loans to Panama, one half of them had at least one Trilateral on their board of directors. Had Panama defaulted on these loans, some major international banks would have faced financial ruin — a scheme had to be implemented to restructure Panama's debts.

So **Sol Linowitz,** director of Marine Midland Bank, was dispatched as "temporary" treaty negotiator (that is, his appointment did not require Senate approval). Again, profit — or the fear of loss of profit — dictated a solution clearly against the majority wishes of the US public, and against its security interests. The Panama Canal Treaty was conflict of interest at its utmost.

Chapter Seven details a new and major development as a direct result of normalization with China: economic trade among countries around the Pacific Ocean has dramatically outstripped its Atlantic counterpart. The Pacific Basin Institute, a think tank to monitor this booming trade and to offer policy "suggestions," is to be located near Scottsdale, Arizona. Away from the hustle and bustle of the West Coast, PBI was proposed by Arizona Governor **Bruce Babitt** and Roger Lyon, president of Valley National Bank of Arizona and formerly a top executive with Chase Manhattan Bank in New York. This chapter is certainly the first critique of PBI, but was possible only because one of the authors of this book also lives in Scottsdale, Arizona and happened to see a reference to it in a local newspaper article.

The next to last chapter probes behind the 1980 presidential election. The evidence declares that Trilaterals were active in all three major campaigns. On the Democratic ticket, **James Carter** and **Walter Mondale** were both members of the Commission. Independent **John Anderson** was also a member. While Republican victor Ronald Reagan was not a member of the Trilateral Commission, many of his top advisors were, like **Caspar Weinberger, David Packard, George Weyerhaeuser, Bill Brock, Anne Armstrong** and others. Two of these received major appointments.

In short, a victory for Reagan is certainly remote from a defeat for Trilateralism. Au contraire, Trilateralism will advance by leaps and bounds under a Reagan administration while a scarce few understand what is really going on.

The last chapter lightly covers European Trilateralism. While this topic could easily take several volumes in itself, we felt it was time to describe and analyze the European counterparts of Trilateralism. We show the link to the European Common Market, central banks and One Europe, and briefly describe Trilateral distribution among the different European countries.

As you may have already noticed, current and former members of the Trilateral Commission appear in bold type throughout this book.

FOOTNOTES, CHAPTER ONE:

1. John Dewey and et.al., *Humanist Manifesto I and II,* p. 16.
2. *Chinese Communist Document,* reproduced in L'Express, November 1, 1980.

CHAPTER TWO

HUMANISM: THE GLOBAL IDEOLOGY

The word *Humanism* is often confused with the concept of *humane-ism*. In fact, however, Humanism is a secular, non-theistic (atheistic) religion that believes man is capable of self-fulfillment, ethical conduct and salvation without supernatural intervention.

Roots of modern-day Humanism go back to at least fifth century B.C. to the Greek philosopher Protagoras who said, "Man is the measure of all things."[1] During the period of the Enlightenment, philosophers such as Jean Jacques Rousseau (1712-1778), Immanuel Kant (1724-1804), Georg Hegel (1770-1831) and slightly later Karl Marx (1818-1883), developed humanistic doctrines that have worked their way into the 20th century in the form of Humanism, Marxism, Socialism, Communism, Collectivism and Rationalism.

Rousseau wrote in *Emile,* "Only through the individual's participation in the 'common unity' can full personal maturity become possible . . . nature is still the norm, but one that has to be recreated, as it were, at a higher level, conferring on man a new rational unity which replaces the purely instinctive unity of the primitive state."[2] In *Du Contrat Social* he proposed a sort of civil religion or civic profession of faith to which every citizen — after giving his free assent — must remain obedient under pain of death.[3]

Hegel coined the idea, "Freedom is not something merely opposed to constraint; on the contrary, it presupposes and requires restraint."[4] Like Rousseau, he contended that the individual could be "free" even when he is being coerced into it, and even though he would not like being forced, he must follow the "public will."

Karl Marx hated Christianity, Judaism and religion in general. He stated: "Criticism of religion is the foundation of all criticism."[5] Even in his own lifetime Marx was known as a militant atheist. All of his writings were directed toward destroying the middle "bourgeois" class by means of the working class, which was to result in a classless society.

At the turn of the century, Humanism was represented in the US by the American Ethical Union. (The American Civil Liberties Union — ACLU — was the legal arm of the AEU.) In 1933 *Humanist Manifesto I* was published in *The New Humanist,* Vol. VI, No. 3, and in 1973 *Humanist Manifesto II* appeared in *The Humanist,* Vol. XXXIII, No. 5.[6]

The following selected quotes from *Humanist Manifesto II* will give you a general idea of its content:

> "*As in 1933, Humanists still believe that traditional theism, especially faith in the prayer-hearing God, assumed to love and care for persons, to hear and understand their prayers, and to be able to do something about them, is an unproved and outmoded faith . . . Reasonable minds look to other means for survival . . . False 'theologies of hope' and messianic ideologies, substituting new dogmas for old, cannot cope with existing world realities . . . No deity will save us, we must save ourselves*".
>
> "*Ethics is autonomous and situational, needing no theological or ideological sanction.*"[7] [Authors' Note: This gave birth to the phrase, "if it feels good, do it."]

"In the area of sexuality, we believe that intolerant attitudes, often cultivated by orthodox religions and puritanical cultures unduly repress sexual conduct".[8]

"We deplore the division of humankind on nationalistic grounds. We have reached a turning point in human history where the best option is to transcend the limits of national sovereignty and to move toward the building of a world community in which all sectors of the human family can participate."

"We believe in the peaceful adjudication of differences by international courts and by the development of the arts of negotiation and compromise. War is obsolete. So is the use of nuclear, biological and chemical weapons."

"The problems of economic growth and development can no longer be resolved by one nation alone; they are worldwide in scope."

"Technology is the vital key to human progress and development."

"We urge that parochial loyalties and inflexible moral and religious ideologies be transcended. Destructive ideological differences among communism, capitalism, socialism, conservatism, liberalism, and radicalism should be overcome."

"[Humanism] . . . transcends the narrow allegiances of church, state, party, class or race in moving toward a wider vision of human potentiality. What more daring a goal for humankind than for each person to become, in ideal as well as practice, a citizen of a world community."[9]

Corliss Lamont is one of the most prolific writers on Humanism, and is literally "Mr. Humanism" in regard to awards, mentions, etc. in humanistic circles. Lamont authored *The Philosophy of Humanism* (1977) and noted "A truly Humanist civilization must be a world civilization."[10] He further wrote:

"Humanism is not only a philosophy with a world ideal, but is an ideal philosophy for the world . . .

*surmounting all national and sectional provincialisms,
provides a concrete opportunity for overcoming the
age-long cleavage between East and West. It is the
philosophic counterpart of world patriotism.[11]*

*"The principle around which the United Nations and
the International Court of Justice are organized is that
the scope of national sovereignty must be curtailed and
that nations must be willing to accept, as against what
they conceived to be their own self-interest, the demo-
cratically arrived at decisions of the world community."[12]*

There is an extraordinary parallelism between Humanists
and Marxists. Among the more obvious are:

- rejection of traditional Christianity and religion
- the necessity for subordination of the individual to state
  and the community
- catchwords of both Humanism and Marxism are "democracy, peace and high standard of living"
- individual rights and beliefs are non-existent
- collectivism is supreme.

CORLISS LAMONT AND THE MORGAN FINANCIAL GROUP

Corliss Lamont (previously quoted as a prime source of
humanist philosophy) is the son of Thomas W. Lamont.

Let's to back to the First World War.

Thomas W. Lamont (1870-1948) was one of the original
organizers of the Round Table group cited by Quigley in
Tragedy and Hope.[13]

Lamont's autobiography is appropriately entitled *Across
World Frontiers.* He was not only a senior partner in J.P.
Morgan & Co., but was also a director of Guaranty Trust
Company, International Harvester Co. (with its Trilateral
directors today) and the law firm of Lamont Corliss & Co.
Thomas Lamont was a key figure in the Morgan financial
group. (For further information and extensive documentation
on the links between J.P. Morgan and the development of the

early Soviet Union, see *Wall Street and the Bolshevik Revolution* by Antony Sutton.)

Mrs. Thomas Lamont was a member of several unusual organizations:

- Federal Union
- American-Russian Institute (on the Attorney General's subversive list)
- National Council of American-Soviet Friendship
- American Committee for Friendship with the Soviet Union . . . and numerous others. (See above citation for full list.)

In short, the Lamont family epitomizes the links between:

- Humanism
- Communism
- New York financial interests

THE ASPEN INSTITUTE FOR HUMANISTIC STUDIES

Humanism today is being "taught" throughout the business world by the Aspen Institute, particularly to the multinational corporation community. The major financiers of Aspen also are the major financiers of Trilateralism, and no less than seven members of the Trilateral Commission also serve at the Aspen Institute.

The Aspen Institute was founded in 1949 by Professor Giuseppe Borgese, Chancellor Robert M. Hutchins (both of University of Chicago) and Walter Paepcke, a Chicago businessman. In 1957, Robert O. Anderson became chairman, and has been its guiding force ever since. In 1969, chairmanship switched to Joseph E. Slater, a member of the Council on Foreign Relations and formerly of the Ford Foundation.

In the past the editors have reported the connections between the Rockefeller Family and the University of Chicago and also between the Ford Foundation and the Trilateral Commission.

The two leading foundations contributing to Aspen are Atlantic-Richfield (ARCO) and the Rockefeller Foundation.

Moreover, the largest single institutional shareholder in ARCO is Chase Manhattan (4.5%) and the largest individual shareholder is Robert O. Anderson, who is also on the board of directors of Chase Manhattan Bank.

FUNDING OF ASPEN INSTITUTE FOR HUMANISTIC STUDIES — 1979 COLORADO

Atlantic Richfield Foundation	$900,000	Long term support
Atlantic Richfield Foundation	250,000	Humanities & Arts Program
Atlantic Richfield Foundation	36,250	Environmental Program
Weyerhaeuser Foundation	15,000	To underwrite planning workshop for project "Consequences of a hypothetical world climate change"
Rockefeller Foundation	150,000	To "bring together estimated and emerging leaders from all sectors of society to discuss and help shape policy by recommendations on contemporary issues"
Rockefeller Foundation	15,000	"Cost of executive seminar on women and men in a changing society"
Rockefeller Foundation	148,000	"Arms control and international security"

SEPTEMBER 1, 1980
WASHINGTON D.C.

Carnegie Corporation	15,000	"Seminar series of Committee for the Third Sector

NEW YORK

Prudential Foundation	10,000	
Ford Foundation	24,395	Conference on student aid policies
Ford Foundation	5,000	Comparative study of state judicial systems
Markle Foundation	220,000	"To provide forum for investigation and discussion of communication in modern society, specifically to investigate relationship between choice in programming content and increasing number of distribution channels for communications"
Rockefeller Brothers Fund	30,000	"Islamic Middle East program"
Kettering Foundation	28,000	"Developing the CEO: educating the integrative leader"

The Markle Foundation (a substantial Aspen backer) is less well known but leads us back to New York banks — in this case to the Morgan Guaranty group. Markle Foundation chairman is Charles F. Biddle, also chairman of the credit policy group of

Morgan Guaranty Trust. Walter H. Page is president of Morgan Guaranty Trust and president of J.P. Morgan. Another director, William M. Rees, is a director of First National City Bank.

In short, it seems the private financing for the Aspen Institute comes from the international banks in New York City, and more specifically, from foundations controlled by Rockefeller and Morgan interests. *Donors support activities which reflect their objectives.*

PUBLIC FINANCING OF ASPEN

In **Brzezinski's** book, *Between Two Ages: America's Role in the Technetronic Era,* he wrote in reference to a proposed constitutional convention, "The needed change is more likely to develop incrementally and less overtly . . . in keeping with the American tradition of blurring distinctions between public and private institutions."[14] A prime Trilateral objective is to blur the distinction between "private" and "public" operations so as to divert public funds into private projects set up by Trilaterals to achieve Trilateral objectives.

A Freedom of Information Act request for information on public financing granted to Aspen was submitted to the National Endowment for the Humanities. We received the following list of NEH grants:

> Ad-20009-80-1434
> PI: Stephen P. Strickland
> Title: Aspen Institute/United Way Bicentennial Project
> Amount: $350,000 G&M (to date $90,000)
> AP-00132-79-1297
> PI: Robert B. McKay
> Title: Development of the Justice Program
> Amount: $15,000 outright
> Grant Period: 11-1-76 to 6-30-80
> CA-28286-77-0616
> PI: Stephen Strickland/Aspen Institute
> Title: Challenge Grant
> Amount: $645,000
> Grant Period: 11-1-76 to 6-30-80[15]

SUMMARY OF ASPEN INSTITUTE FUNDING

In brief, Aspen Institute has been funded from the following sources, taking 1979 as a representative year:

U.S. Taxpayer (via National Endowment for the Humanities)	$1,010,000
Atlantic Richfield Foundation	1,186,250
Rockefeller Foundation 343,000	
Markle Foundation (Morgan Financial interests	220,000
Other Foundations	97,000
TOTAL	$2,856,000

The key point to note is the heavy representation of donations that have also financed Trilateralism: these include Weyerhaeuser, Rockefeller, Ford and Kettering.

THE ASPEN EXECUTIVE SEMINAR PROGRAM

While central offices of Aspen are in New York City, it has "centers of activity" (i.e. seminar and housing facilities) in Washington, D.C., Cambridge, Princeton, New Haven, Boulder, Hawaii, Tokyo and Berlin.

According to an Aspen publication:

"The idea behind the Aspen Institute has three essential ingredients: to gather thoughtful men and women around the table, not across the table; to explore the power of ideas in great literature stretching from ancient to contemporary time, and to translate ideas into policies and actions that meet the challenge of our age. [Emhasis added.]

"In view of the rapidly increasing worldwide activities of the Institute, its international Board of Trustees and key staff act on the Institute's long-standing principle to maintain absolute control over the selection of individual participants and their mix in all its meetings, the

locations at which its meetings are held, as well as the subjects to be discussed."[16]

At these meetings, a hotchpotch of corporate executives, military people, intellectuals and media personages "mingle" and become "educated," typically for a period of two weeks at a time. This subtle form of brainwashing on global affairs is coupled with the breaking down of hard line principled positions through peer pressure. As Wilbur Mills once said, "To get along you have to go along."

This is quite successful. For example, Newsweek reports that Bill Moyers (a special adviser to Aspen Institute) has drawn more than ten of his Public Broadcasting Service programs from contacts and ideas developed at Aspen.[17] PBS is supported by many of the same foundations that support the Aspen Institute and Trilateralism in addition to large amounts of *public money* (Corporation for Public Broadcasting, etc.). Once again we observe a "blurring" of institutions where elitists combine their money with public financing to achieve their own ends and spread their global propaganda.

THE FUND FOR GOVERNANCE

According to the Institute's *A Brief Overview:*

"...the Institute is undertaking a sustained examination of crucial issues of Governance: how societies and their governments and institutions, public and private, national and international, can better respond to the often conflicting pressures for social justice, fairness, efficiency and individual freedom. Under this broad theme of Governance, the Institute focuses on such subjects as Financing the Future; Human Rights; The Corporation and Society; Energy; A Challenge to Governance; Tradition and Modernization; The First 20 Years of Life; Ethics; Religion and Governance; Work, Industrial Policy and Society; and Structures for Peace. While these issues of Governance will be pursued throughout the year and around the globe, the preeminent setting for the dealing with Governance questions is

the Institute's newly acquired Wye Plantation outside of Washington, D.C."[18]

Why should the Aspen Institute undertake this program? It merely quotes from Edmund Burke, "The only thing necessary for the triumph of evil is for good men to do nothing."[19] Apparently the Institute equates itself with the "good men."

The Institute proposes to raise about $15 million for operating capital for this project. An annual budget of at least $1.2 million will provide a staff of senior fellows and consultants (about $450,000 per year) with workshops, seminars and consultative sessions and publications costing about $600,000 a year.

The Atlantic Richfield Company provided the first grant of $1 million and it is anticipated that another $3 million will be raised from corporations and foundations. As much as $6 million could come from *public* funds — either congressional appropriations or through the National Endowment for the Humanities grants.

Some of the participants in this program will not surprise you: Harlan Cleveland, John Gardner, Trilateral **Henry Kissinger,** Marion Doenhoff and Pehr Gyllenhammar.

Without question, this Aspen program is a well-funded attack on Constitutional America.

CONCLUSIONS

- Humanism is a man-centered, atheistic religion inconsistent with and indeed utterly opposed to traditional Christianity, Biblical theology or Orthodox Judaism.
- The philosophy has been nurtured and promoted by the same group of globalists that nurtures and supports communism.
- Humanism is intimately connected with Trilateralism, and calls for the elimination of nationalism and nationalistic boundaries.
- Trilateral-style Humanism is procreated primarily by The Aspen Institute, and is funded by taxpayers' money as well as by private foundation and corporate funds.

FOOTNOTES CHAPTER 2

1. Protagoras, *Protagoras IV*, 51.
2. J.J. Rousseau, *Emile*.
3. ———, *Du Contrat Social*.
4. Paul Edwards, *Encyclopedia of Philosophy*.
5. Ibid.
6. Both of these Manifestos are available from Prometheus Books, 923 Kensington Avenue, Buffalo, New York 14215.
7. John Dewey et al, *Humanist Manifesto I and II*, p. 14-16.
8. Ibid., p. 17, 18.
9. Ibid., p. 21-23.
10. Corliss Lamont, *The Philosophy of Humanism*, p. 281.
11. Ibid., p. 282, 283.
12. Ibid., p. 257, 258.
13. Ibid.
14. Zbigniew Brzezinski, *Between Two Ages: America's Role in the Technetronic Era*, p. 259.
15. *Report of Financing Granted to Aspen Institute*, National Endowment for the Humanities, 14th report (1979).
16. *The Aspen Institute: a Brief Overview*, Aspen Institute.
17. Eric Gelman, *The Great American Salon*, Newsweek XCVI (July 14, 1980), p. 66.
18. Aspen Institute, Op. Cit.
19. Edmund Burke, *Letter to William Smith*, January 9, 1795.

CHAPTER THREE

GLOBAL SCHOOLING: THE RE-EDUCATION OF AMERICA

> *"National security today involves more than military preparation. Global education is one of the essential new dimensions.*
>
> *"The globalization of the human condition is interweaving the destinies of all nations and peoples at an accelerating rate and affecting many aspects of life. Global education involves multidisciplinary perspectives about the extended human family, the existing condition of mankind and the planet, and foreseeable consequences of present trends and alternative choices."[1]*

Note that the above was written by Robert Leestma of the U.S. Office of Education, a contributor to the 1979 book, *Schooling for a Global Age* (See bibliography).

While the previous chapter detailed the religion of Humanism and its thrust behind Trilateralism, this chapter seeks to document a massive re-education program of American school-age children — and unwilling parents, who remain a major obstable to a smooth transition to a global society.

On the back dust cover of the above quoted book, it is noted:

> *"This book is one of a series of three books on issues and practices in schooling. The other two books deal with the arts and education and with school-community relations. The series was commissioned to provide background information for A Study of Schooling in the United States, the results of which will be published subsequently."[2]*

Also noted are the financial backers of the studies:

The Danforth Foundation
The John D. Rockefeller III Fund
Martha Holden Jennings Foundation
Charles F. Kettering Foundation
Charles Stewart Mott Foundation
The Needmor Fund
The Rockefeller Foundation
The Spencer Foundation
U.S. Office of Education
National Institute of Education[3]

Emphasis is added to note two things: first, the Rockefeller and Kettering foundations originally funded the Trilateral Commission. Second, public funds are intermixed with private funds to facilitate and implement a non-public supported or authorized endeavor.

We have chosen to analyze *Schooling for a Global Age* because of its authority of scholarship, financial backing and impact. It is not an *"official"* US government publication, but government officials are quoted and substantial government funds were provided so the study could be undertaken.

In light of this, we can be sure the book typifies the thinking of the National Education Association (NEA), the Department of Education, the various foundations listed and most importantly, the thinking of **David Rockefeller** et al.

A PHILOSOPHY OF EDUCATION FOR WORLD CITIZENSHIP

Keeping in mind the last chapter dealing with Humanism, the following *"purpose statement"* exemplifies the Humanist philosophy on global education:

- *"To develop student understanding of themselves as individuals.*
- *"To develop student understanding of themselves as members of the human species.*
- *"To develop student understanding of themselves as inhabitants and dependents of planet Earth.*
- *"To develop student understanding of themselves as participants in global society.*
- *"To develop within students the competencies required to live intelligently and responsibly as individuals, human beings, earthlings, and members of global society.*

  ". . . We endeavor to create in world-centered schools the kind of social order, the organizational climate, the physical environment, and the formal curriculum that support and further the purposes of global education."⁴

  "Identities, loyalties, and competencies as well as rights, duties, obligations, and privileges are associated with each of these goals. For example, students might explore the issues involved and discuss the rights one has by virtue of being a member of the human species. The Universal Declaration of Human Rights, the Humanist Manifesto, and UNICEF and the Rights of the Child are among many documents and other materials which can be used in considering this question."⁵

According to Irving H. Buchen, the student *". . . will be capable of sustaining many allegiances, without contradiction, on both a national and international scale, and be closer to being, especially through the concept of global perspectives, a world citizen."⁶*

The Aspen Institute for Humanistic Studies paper, *American Education and Global Interdependence,* states:

  "The educational enterprise has a vital role to play in

preparing present and future generations of Americans to cope with interdependence. Universities contain intellectual skills needed to develop the knowledge base about global interdependence; developing a more secure knowledge base should facilitate greatly the building of political consensus on what we should do about global interdependence.

The mass media by their very nature are event-centered, imposing on schools and colleges an obligation to provide students with the continuity and depth of understanding demanded by complex long-term interdependence issues.

Schools, furthermore, have the golden opportunity, if they will but use it, of shaping the world views of future generations of Americans along lines more compatible with the realities of global interdependence before these views become hardened through maturation along other less compatible lines."[7]

Global education requires the conversion of existing local educational systems — primarily those at the elementary and secondary school levels — to produce students who see themselves not as Americans but as participants in a world society.

Why? Because *"nationalism"* and *"individualism"* are lumped in with the *"other less compatible lines."*

Society must be planned, they say, in overt and covert ways; individual ethnic, cultural and intellectual differences will be subordinated to some predetermined set of characteristics set forth by the elitist group preparing us for global interdependence.

AN ACTION PLAN IS UNDERWAY

The Aspen Institute study noted, *"The task of bringing about the kind of transformation which will make education a better instrument for coping with interdependence is formidable."*[8] To achieve their plan, global educators propose to identify and concentrate action upon what they call *"critical leverage points"* in our present educational system.

The plan is to subvert and change these critical points into a program to achieve global goals. When analyzed, Aspen's six point plan of action is nothing less than cultural genocide:

> *"Point 1: Revise curricula, the content of teacher training and community education toward global education. It is proposed to use the U.S. Department of Education as well as independent foundations and local school systems for this purpose.*
>
> *Point 2: To obtain support from political and educational leaders at both national and local levels, particularly from boards of trustees and professional organizations, to mold public support for global education.*
>
> *Point 3: To use universities and research institutions to develop a "knowledge base" on interdependence in order to help build the political consensus necessary for global policies.*
>
> *Point 4: To shape existing world outlooks within American popular culture.*
>
> *Point 5: To reach outward to the world through educational institutes, particularly through the United Nations.*
>
> *Point 6: To influence mass media to these ends, particularly through the use of internships that are part of professional training in mass communications."*[9]
>
> (Authors' note: there are many college-age students who have been raised in prototype *"global schools"* who think in global terms and can be *"interned"* in strategic places within the media.)

Aspen makes it clear that this is an *activist* plan: *"Achieving the educational transformation, which the future demands will require all of the spirit of conquest and aspiration which we possess."*[10]

CENTRALIZED, GOVERNMENT-CONTROLLED EDUCATION REQUIRED

Globalists recognize that American education is essentially decentralized and that public education has historically played a role in the teaching of American history and government. Thus, one objective is to heavily reduce the amount of time devoted to the study of these subjects now required in the curricula of most states. These America-oriented curricula will be replaced with ones concentrating on world history and politics.

They describe the current educational system as a *"constitutional incongruity."* Certain constitutional conflicts do exist which cannot be overcome as long as education remains in the hands of local and state governments. A major answer to this was the creation of the Department of Education, which was heavily lobbied by the global-minded National Education Association (NEA).

The Aspen study also cited Roger Ulrich's *The Control of Human Behavior.* According to Ulrich, conditioning is supposed to start at the age of two years.[11] It is recognized within the global education community that the critical years for the establishment of values and ideas is around seven to twelve. Consequently, it is planned to subject students to a curricula which employs behavioral techniques involving so-called *"values clarification"* and situational ethics.

This manipulates students into an artificial belief structure. Who picks the values they will be taught? Which set of ethics will be used?

These techniques are close to those of Goebbels' in Nazi Germany, or Soviet and Chinese propagandists of today. These are programs for human behavioristic manipulation, not education!

THE PLAN IS UNDERWAY

Don't make the mistake of underestimating the forces behind global schooling. This is not some passive, *"pie-in-the-sky"* ideological exercise of academia — it is highly organized, completely funded and well staffed. It is sweeping the country.

The following *"timetable"* is quoted *exactly* from pages 240-241 of *Schooling for a Global Age.*

"PHASE 1, PREPARATORY PERIOD — BY 1980:
* *Every state education department and most school systems and teacher education programs would have a*

collection of some basic references on global education and would have provided opportunities for selected staff members to become aware of the global education concept, some relevant research, successful programs elsewhere, and local possibilities.

- *In-service education programs would be available in every region of the country to begin to acquaint teachers and others with the global education concept.*

- *A survey of the role of the world in the community, region, or state and vice versa would have been conducted, planned, or under consideration in a majority of states.*

"PHASE 2 - BY THE MID-1980s:

- *Study groups would be at work in a sizeable proportion of state education departments, local school systems, and teacher education institutions to analyze and enrich existing curricula, requirements, and materials from a global perspective.*

- *In-service education opportunities would be available in the majority of states, including through teacher centers.*

- *Pre-service education programs would be offering some orientation to global education, at least as an option.*

- *Initial research agendas would be established and studies and surveys begun.*

- *A national baseline survey of the knowledge and attitudes of students, teachers, administrators, parents, and community leaders on global education concerns would be completed.*

- *Every state education department and a sizeable proportion of school districts would become involved in an international educational exchange program for students and/or staff.*

- *State and local school board policy statements would be giving explicit support to global education.*

- *National public awareness and local community support would be growing, in part, because of increased*

attention to global problems and issues in the mass media, particularly television, and in the schools.
"PHASE 3 - BY 1990:

- *Teachers in every state would have access to in-service education programs for global education, at least at the awareness level.*

- *Good case-study material on the initiation or improvement of global education programs in a variety of school and community situations would be becoming widely available.*

- *All school districts, state education departments, and pre-service teacher-education programs would have access to information clearinghouses and resource centers on global perspectives in education.*

- *Teacher certification requirements in a sizeable number of states would begin to reflect global education concerns.*

- *State curriculum requirements in a sizeable number of states would begin to reflect global education objectives.*

- *School accreditation requirements would begin to reflect attention to global education.*

- *Local, state, and national assessments of educational progress would include attention to global educational concerns.*

- *Textbooks and other educational materials would increasingly provide more adequate treatment of global issues and perspectives."[12]*

PARENTS NEED TO BE EDUCATED ALSO

John I. Goodlad wrote in *Schooling for a Global Age:*
"Parents and the general public must be reached also. Otherwise, children and youth enrolled in globally oriented programs may find themselves in conflict with values assumed in the home. And then the educational institution frequently comes under scrutiny and must pull back."[13]

The question basically boils down to this: *"Are your values good enough for your children, or not?"* We have passed through the UN-sponsored "International Year of the Child" which preached children's rights. In Sweden it is now against the law to spank your own child —who could report *you* to the authorities for *"maltreatment."*

This thought is expanded:

> *"Parents should understand that developing independent individuals is not a goal of government education, and this becomes apparent only with an understanding of the educator's view of an individual: 'The emerging modern individual places his confidence not in society's norms, not religion's rules, nor parents' dictates, but in his own changing experience. He is, in a very deep sense, his own highest authority. He chooses his own way.'"[14]*

The greatest obstacle to the implementing of global schooling is not lack of funding, trained teachers or global textbooks — it is the *parent* who is skeptical about the federal government (with its blurred distinctions between private and public institutions) being better qualified to say how his child should be raised and educated.

"Rebel" parents who have chosen to educate their children at home have become *"examples"* to globalists who drag the parents into court on civil and criminal charges of negligence.

Private schools across the country have continuously fought an onslaught of legislation that would destroy them, if passed. Whenever a student is transfered to a private school, the public school he or she attended loses state and federal budget funds for the following year. In many cases, the formula for determining funding is disproportionate to the total number of students in attendance; thus, if 40% of the students withdrew to private schools, those schools could lose 70 or 80% of its funding. This is intolerable to public educators, and pressure is put on the parent to re-enroll the student in public school.

One of the key activist groups that deals with parent as well as student problems is the National Education Association (NEA); possibly it is the most powerful special interest group in operation today. The NEA sent more delegates to the Democratic National Convention in 1980 than *any* other interest group including trade unions.

The NEA worked closely with the Trilaterally oriented **Carter** administration in setting up the long sought after Federal Department of Education to centralize US education.

A national movement was recently underway to pass legislation allowing tuition tax credits for parents of students enrolled in private schools. This is not surprising in that they are paying for two educations at the same time — private *and* public. If passed, it would have dealt a fatal blow to global educators because it would have encouraged parents to seek better, private education for their children; in turn, public schools would have their funding automatically chopped. The National Education Association was successful at blocking this legislation.

HOW GLOBAL EDUCATION IS BEING FINANCED

We noted earlier that the Aspen Institute for Humanistic Studies is funded primarily by Atlantic Richfield, Rockefeller, Kettering, Weyerhaeuser, Ford and the Markle Foundations. In addition, we saw that almost 40% of Aspen's funding came from the National Endowment for the Humanities (NEH).

NEH granted a whopping total of $185.3 million in 1979 to many different Humanistic and globalist endeavors, including Aspen Institute. While the US taxpayer contributes about 80% of NEH's annual funding, the remaining 20% comes from Lilly Endowment, the Ford Foundation and the Andrew W. Mellon and Alfred P. Sloan Foundations.

Watchers of the Public Broadcasting System will see many global-oriented shows sponsored by Ford Foundation.

The Kettering Foundation, a main backer of the Trilateral Commission, has as its purpose statement: *"To strengthen the mechanisms for citizen participation in public policy formation and implementation, and to support the forces for world order and peace. It supports only innovative, high-risk programs which do not receive sufficient attention from other sources."[15]*

Table 1 gives you an idea of what Kettering considers *"innovative, high risk."*

TABLE I

SELECTED CHARLES F. KETTERING FOUNDATION

Academy for Contemporary Problems ($80,000)
Columbus, OH 1/1/79. To jointly develop and sponsor project, National Urban Policy Roundtable, to establish discussion framework for a *coordinated national urban policy.*

Action For a Better Community ($9,300)
Rochester, NY. 2/15/79. For handbook, *How to Develop an Insurance Cooperative,* and to identify settings in which cooperative development would provide alternative to disruptive market forces at the neighborhood level.

Aspen Institute for Humanistic Studies ($28,000)
NYC, NY. 1/15/78. 2-year grant. To cosponsor studies and seminars on economic modernization in the People's Republic of China.

Cornell University ($24,000)
Department of Human Development and Family Studies, Ithaca, NY. 11/15/78. For project Ecology of Human Development, studying *child development* in relation to child care; education, and family support system policies and practices.

National League of Cities ($100,000)
DC. 12/15/78. For program with U.S. Civil Service Commission Bureau of Intergovernmental Personnel Programs to improve *group skills and policy management systems* of municipal policy makers in selected demonstrations cities, and *to develop national network of trainers of elected officials.*

Policy Sciences Center ($40,000)
NYC, NY. 2/13/78. To develop process for *direct unofficial discussion* between multinational corporations and less developed countries' leaders.

Stanford University ($29,376)
U.S. - China Relations Program, Stanford, CA. 9/1/78. To continue project, Technology Policy and Development in People's Republic of China, focusing on areas of research and development for food production and telecommunications in China.[16]

We noted earlier that Kettering was a supporter of *Schooling for a Global Age.* That book also states, *"Substudy on the teaching of global education in schools [is] supported by an additional grant from the Charles F. Kettering Foundation."*[17] (Emphasis added.)

Among the Kettering directorship, we find two notable Humanists: George Gallup and Norman Cousins. Cousins is a director of National Educational Television and the U.N. Association of the U.S. Gallup surveys, which are supposed to be so *"unbiased,"* are usually called for when globalists want to *"prove"* their case to the public by doing a public opinion survey.

While the authors have not done an exhaustive tabulation on the amount of money distributed by public and private institutions for globalist ends, it is estimated that well over $1 billion per year is sunk into *"high risk"* programs that would otherwise find *no support.*

MASS MEDIA AND THE MARKLE FOUNDATION

The Markle Foundation was identified as a prime contributor to the Aspen Institute and ties to the Morgan banking establishment were noted in the previous chapter.

Markle's statement of purpose reads: *"The goal of the current program is to strengthen educational uses of the mass media and communications technology."*[18]

This foundation deserves extra space as a prime purveyor of global education. The president of Markle Foundation is Lloyd N. Morrisett. Over ten years ago, when Morrisett was a vice-president of Carnegie Corporation, he and Joan Cooney (wife of Trilateralist **Peter G. Peterson**) originated the idea for *Sesame Street.* He is currently chairman of the board of trustees at *Children's Television Workshop,* which produces Sesame Street.

According to the 1978 Annual Report of the Markle Foundation:

"In its first operating year, 1969-1970, the Workshop had 36 employees and a budget of $6.8 million. Almost all this money came from three sources: The Office of Education, the Carnegie Corporation of New York, and the Ford Foundation. The Workshop itself was able to provide only $119,000 from its own income."[19]

It later stated that:

"CTW has established its status as a public charity under the Tax Reform Act of 1969. The value of the public charity classification to an organization such as CTW is that it allows the receipt of individual or corporate contributions on a fully tax deductible basis for the donor. It also facilitates philanthropic donations by foundations."[20]

Which foundations contribute to support Sesame Street so it can stay on the air? Surprisingly, not Markle Foundation, even though they are closely linked. Markle spends its funds on more *"high risk"* ventures just starting out (see Table II).

What is interesting to see is that these ventures, like Sesame Street, were persistently bailed out financially, year after year, because they could not make their own way. Further, major funds to this end came from *your* taxes, as well as various foundations.

CONCLUSIONS:

- A main tenet of Humanism is to institute global education to create a generation of "global citizens."
- Global education is being financed by the same foundations that finance Humanism and the Trilateral Commission.
- Massive amounts of public funds are also being used to these ends.
- There is a plan, a timetable, sufficient personnel and funds to carry out the plan.
- Global education ideology is in direct conflict with the Constitution of the United States.

TABLE II

1975

65,213 to Cable Arts Foundation. For development of arts programming on cable television.

$35,000 to Rand Corporation, Communications Policy Program. For beginning research to identify and measure the size of special interest audiences for public television.

$112,000 to University of California, School of Medicine, Laboratory for the Study of Human Interaction & Conflict, Phychiatric Department. For field study of the effects of television on children.

$92,298 to University of Minnesota, School of Journalism and Mass Communication, Communication Research Division. To pursue research on ways in which children are influenced by pro-social television content.

1976

$2,500 to The Rand Corporation. Support of the publication and distribution of a study on new evaluation methods for "Sesame Street" and "The Electric Company."

$29,380 to the University of Wisconsin, Mass Communications Research Center. Support of a study of the influence of mass communications on young voters.

1977

$14,189 to American Assembly. To sponsor an American Assembly to discuss the ways the mass media in the United States shapes the politics of Presidential selection.

$170,000 to Aspen Institute. Support of Aspen Program on Communications and Society.

$19,425 to Cultural Council Foundation. Support for Independent Cinema Artists and Producers to act as a distributor with pay television systems for independent film and video artists.

$70,887 to Harvard University. Two studies to examine how children come to understand the television medium and the steps where they learn to make distinction between fantasy and reality.[21]

FOOTNOTES CHAPTER 3
1. Robert Leestma, *Schooling for a Global Age,* ed. James M. Becker, p. 233.
2. Ibid., Dust cover.
3. Ibid., Dust cover.
4. Lee and Charlotte Anderson, Op. cit., pg. 8.
5. James Becker, Op. cit., pg. 41.
6. Irving Buche, *Learning for Tomorrow,* ed. Alvin Toffler, p. 137.
7. *American Education and Global Interdependence,* Aspen Institute.
8. Ibid.
9. Ibid.
10. Ibid.
11. Roger Ulrich, *Control of Human Behavior.*
12. Robert leestman, Op. cit., p. 240, 241.
13. John I. Goodlad, Ibid., 17.
14. Carl Rogers, *Courses by Newspaper.*
15. *Charles F. Kettering Foundation Annual Report, 1979.*
16. Ibid., p. 36.
17. James Becker, Op.cit., p. vii.
18. *Markle Foundation Annual Report* (1977), p. 4.
19. Ibid., p. 8.
20. Ibid., p. 17.
21. Ibid., p. 58-65.

CHAPTER FOUR

TRANSCENDING POLITICAL SYSTEMS: CAPITALISTS VS. MARXISTS

One of the most pervasive — but downright erroneous — themes in modern textbook history is that of a competition between Capitalist and Marxist systems. In fact, given objective examination of all facts nothing could be further from the truth. The two political power groups cooperate with each other, nurture each other and in general are jointly responsible for much of the pain and suffering of the average man on the street in this world.

Much of the confusion stems from an unwillingness to define monopoly capitalism for what it is: a political power system that is much like state socialism. State socialism, as in the Soviet Union, is also remarkably akin in its operations to that of a monopoly. Thus, a Brezhnev and a Rockefeller have much in common. Both are monopolists and both thrive on use of political power to retain their monopoly.

With this parallel in mind, let's summarize the facts on the almost continuous involvement of American elitist capitalists in the buildup of Soviet military power over the past 63 years. It has been a deliberate policy. That it was done shortsightedly for financial gain is rather obvious. No one — not even a multinational businessman — commits suicide knowingly, but it is not unheard of for avarice to overcome common sense.

Apparently only one US institution has been clearsighted on the buildup of Soviet power. *From the early 1920's until recently only one institution has spoken out.* That institution is the AFL-CIO. From Samuel Gompers in 1920 down to George Meany, major unions consistently protested the trade policies that built the Soviet military power. Why? Because workers in Russia lost their freedom with the Bolshevik Revolution, and the products used to expedite the killing of union members in Korea and Vietnam were made with the help of American elitist controlled multinational company technology. *But today Trilateral Commissioner Kirkland rules the AFL-CIO and the protest is muted.*

THE BOLSHEVIK REVOLUTION (1917)

The March, 1917, Russian Revolution overthrew the regime of the Romanov Czars and installed a free, constitutional government. In November the fledgling republic was destroyed by the totalitarian Bolsheviks and the Russian hope for freedom evaporated. The powerful American elite was involved because *Wall Street financiers* and attorneys intervened in support of the Bolsheviks. A few examples of this support are:

- Key Wall Streeters assisting the Bolsheviks included William Boyce Thompson (director of Chase National, forerunner of Chase Manhattan), Albert H. Wiggin (president of Chase Bank), establishment attorneys and Morgan bankers.

- The Wall Street bankers pressured the US and British governments to support Bolsheviks, much as **Rockefeller** and **Kissinger** pressured **Carter** into admitting the Shah of Iran into the US in 1979. *The Wall Street pressures were to assist Bolshevik propaganda, encourage formation of a Soviet army and supply arms to the Bolsheviks.*

- Some statements by American elitist businessmen on the early Soviets include the following letter from William Saunders, chairman of Ingersoll-Rand Corporation, to President Wilson, on October 17, 1918:

  "Dear Mr. President: I am in sympathy with the Soviet form of government as that best suited for the Russian people."[1]

- And another from Thomas D. Thacher, Wall Street attorney and member of the establishment law firm Simpson, Thacher & Bartlett (former Secretary of State **Vance** is today a member of this same firm):

  ". . .The fullest assistance should be given to the Soviet government in its efforts to organize a volunteer revolutionary army."[2]

Wall Street bankers, including Chase National bankers, aided the Bolshevik Revolution by intervention with the United States and British governments and were crucial to its success.

THE EARLY YEARS OF SOVIET RUSSIA

Wall Street then came to the aid of the newborn Soviet government. Armand Hammer (now chairman of the Occidental Petroleum Corporation) received the first concession contract in 1920 because his father, Julius Hammer, was then Secretary of the Communist Party in the US. However, the Rockefellers were not far behind. Under the guidance of Reeve Schley (a Chase VP) the American-Russian Chamber of Commerce was formed in partnership with Russian agents to break the U.S. government ban on trade with the Soviets.

What could not be done legally was done illegally — even to the export of military aircraft engines. *By the late 1920's Wall Street and German bankers had put the infant Soviet Russia on its feet.*

In 1925, a complete program to finance imports of Soviet raw material to the United States and to export vital machinery and technology to the Soviets was agreed upon by Chase National and Prombank (a German bank).

At the same time — even though a government ban still

existed on all trade with the Soviet Union — Chase National was trying to arrange for export of Liberty motors for military planes. Years later, when writing *Western Technology and Soviet Economic Development,* the co-author (Sutton) found the evidence in State Department files and learned that the Department of Justice was one step ahead of Chase National and intervened to stop illegal exports.

Along with Equitable Trust, Chase National was in the forefront of financing Soviet economic and military development in the 1920's. When acceptance of gold was halted by the State Department, the Chase-Soviet business was arranged on the basis of platinum credits.

Above all, the formation of the American-Russian Chamber of Commerce, with Chase VP Reeve Schley as its president, was the major factor in circumventing the ban on US technology for the Soviet Union. The Chamber was active in pressing the need for "cooperation" and "peaceful trade." The Chamber representative in Moscow was none other than Charles Haddell Smith, previously in Soviet employ and a member of the Soviet Peasant International.

By the late 1920's, Chase was even attempting to raise loans for the Soviets in the US, the first being a $30 million deal with principal and interest, payable in dollars — flatly prohibited by State Department regulations.

We also find in State Department files, letters from Chase refusing to break off the illegal relationship when instructed to do so. Public comment at that time was more caustic than in today's tame media. Chase was called — among the more delicate descriptions — "an international fence," "a disgrace to America. . .They will go to any lengths for a few dollars profit."[3]

This intimate link between Chase National (which became Chase Manhattan in the 1950's) and the Soviets is unbroken throughout six decades.

THE FIRST FIVE YEAR PLANS (1930-45)

In 1930, Chase National was one of four American banks that financed construction of the Five-Year Plans (master plans devised to expedite economic expansion through rapid industrialization of the once largely agricultural society) and, according to State Department files, its advisor was Soviet agent Alexander Ginsberg. In 1930, according to the U.S. Treasury, *all* Soviet accounts were with the Chase National Bank. Today the principal Chase Manhattan correspondent bank in Russia is Narodny Bank.

The Five-Year Plans have been hailed in the history books as a triumph of Soviet engineering. In fact, the Plans were entirely packaged and implemented by non-Russian companies — mostly American — for the profit of Wall Street. Rockefeller interests received a large portion of the money that flowed from this initial effort to modernize the Soviet Union. This included its war industries, ammunition, modern aircraft, tanks and warships.

WORLD WAR II

Lend Lease (the US program offering assistance to the Allies during World War II) provided the means for the Soviets to resist Nazi aggression. The Soviet Union was the recipient of the latest in US military technology during World War II — once again for the profit of large US multinationals.

POST WORLD WAR II

The buildup of Soviet economic and military power has continued from 1945 down to the present day under the guise of peaceful trade.

A good example is the truck industry: any truck plant that produces civilian trucks can also produce military trucks. All Soviet automobile, truck and engine technology comes from the West, and chiefly from the United States. The Soviet military has over 300,000 trucks — the bulk of which came from these US-built plants.

Up to 1968 the largest motor vehicle plant in the USSR was at Gorki — and it was built by the Ford Motor Company and the Austin Company as a part of so-called "peaceful trade." The Gorki plant produced many of the trucks American pilots saw on the Ho Chi Minh Trail. The chassis for the GAZ-69 rocket launcher used against Israel was also produced there, along with the Soviet jeep and half a dozen other military vehicles.

In 1968, while the Gorki plant was building vehicles to be used in Vietnam and against Israel, further equipment for the plant was ordered and shipped from the US.

Also in 1968 there was the so-called "Fiat deal" — a plan to build a plant at Volgograd three times bigger than the one at Gorki. Dean Rusk and Walter Rostow told Congress and the American public this was "peaceful trade," that the Fiat plant could not produce military vehicles. However, as previously stated, *any* automobile manufacturing plant can produce military vehicles. The main design contract for the Volgograd plant was held by Fiat, whose chairman was soon-to-be Trilateral **Giovanni Agnelli. Agnelli** is also on the International Advisory Committee of Chase Manhattan Bank (The IAC chairman is **Henry Kissinger**).

Fiat in Italy doesn't make automobile manufacturing equipment; they use U.S. manufactured equipment. Fiat did send 1,000 men to Russia for the erection of the plant — but over half of the equipment came from the United States, namely Gleason Works, TRW Inc. of Cleveland, U.S. Industries. Inc. and New Britain Machine Co.

So in the middle of a war that killed 46,000 Americans and countless Vietnamese with Soviet weapons and supplies, Trilaterals doubled Soviet auto output.

In 1972, the Soviets received equipment and technology from the West to build the largest heavy truck plant in the world — the Kama plant — to produce 100,000 ten-ton trucks per year — more than produced by *all* US manufacturers put together. It is also the largest plant in the world, covering over 36 square miles.

Does the Kama truck plant have military potential? The Soviets themselves answered this one. The Kama-produced truck is rated 60 per cent higher than the ZIL-130 truck, and the ZIL series trucks are standard Soviet army trucks used in Vietnam, the Middle East and Afghanistan.

In the opening paragraphs of this chapter we quoted the support from William Saunders, chairman of Ingersoll-Rand, for the Bolsheviks in 1918. Today we find the same firm

Ingersoll-Rand aiding the military buildup of the Soviet Union for military equipment in use by the Soviets. According to *Business Week*:

> *"Meanwhile, a smaller but politically still more inflammatory shipment is also rolling — toward Russia's Kama River truck plant. New Jersey's Ingersoll-Rand Co. expects to complete by late this year an $8.8 million order of automated production-line equipment used to make diesel engines at the Soviet manufacturing which produced trucks used in the invasion of Afghanistan. The shipments are authorized under the Commerce Department's general licenses, not yet under strict controls."[4]*

The pro-Soviet stance of American businessmen today, as well as in 1918, is well typified by Dresser Industries. The company is now finishing a drill bit plant worth $146 million at Kuibyshev. The Soviets need high-quality drill bits to step up oil exploration, and oil is needed to fuel its overseas expansion program.

Dresser has not only continued to press ahead with the plant, but is attempting to keep its Soviet role quiet to avoid public backlash in the US. To quote Dresser's senior vice-president Edward R. Luter:

> *"Dresser is keeping a low profile on the plant. We're not looking for any publicity, because we're afraid if our name comes up, and the project is called to people's attention, they might remember that they wanted to do something to stop it. We hope we can let sleeping dogs lie, and let things continue to roll."[5]*

The reason that Dresser wants to keep its role from the public is simple: according to Department of Defense expert Dr. William Perry the Soviets "will be able to detect and monitor all US subs using oil exploration equipment sold to them by the US."[6]

KISSINGER AND SOVIET MILITARY BUILD UP

Henry Kissinger has been intimately connected for two decades with the Rockefeller family as a family advisor —

before going to Washington in 1970. In the March 1979 issue of *The Trilateral Observer* the annual cash payments from Nelson Rockefeller to **Henry Kissinger were listed from 1958 to 1969 (Kissinger** entered the White House as National Security Advisor to President Nixon in 1969).[7] Each year, cash payments averaging at least $12,000 were made to **Henry Kissinger**. An official report on these transactions concluded that the payments "were for work done for the family rather than on a consulting basis through any governmental agency."[8] **Kissinger** can be described as the intellectual hired hand of the Rockefellers. **Kissinger** was responsible for brushing aside information that our exports to the Soviets had military potential and for forcing US government officials to approve export of equipment with military potential.

The co-author's (Sutton) personal knowledge of the role of **David Packard** (later Secretary of Defense, from 1969 to 1971) in suppressing information of military potential, and the intimate relations of **David Rockefeller** and **Henry Kissinger**, suggests that the Trilateral group was the origin of the 1970's phase to profit from the building of the military power of the Soviet Union.

Kissinger's personal role can be gleaned from documents leaked to columnist Jack Anderson, which read in part:

> *"At the time (1972) some officials, including then Secretary of Defense, Melvin Laird, voiced concern that the Russians might use the central Asian truck plant — the biggest in the world — to produce military equipment."*[9]

Kissinger brushed the misgivings aside. A confidential Commerce Department memorandum states that in 1971 **Kissinger** "ordered the Secretary of Commerce to grant three pending applications" for construction of the Soviet plant.[10] Another secret memo set the final value of US-licensed equipment and technology at $1.5 billion. Others — notably our Western European allies —were not so sure. On March 20, 1975, **Kissinger** cabled US officials in Paris on the best way to quiet such doubts. "Kama trucks are not tactical military vehicles with cross-country capabilities," the secret cable said. "Some may ultimately be outfitted with front-wheel drive for muddy or icy environment. However, trucks will not be equipped for deep fording or have other features typical of military models." Kissinger's cable concluded that "we see little likelihood of diversion to military uses"[12] even though there was ample evidence on file in Washington that diversion to military uses would be made.

THE TRILATERAL VIEW OF COMMUNISM

In the light of the above material it becomes critical to know the Trilateral opinion of Communism.

In *Triangle Paper No. 13, Collaboration with Communist Countries in Managing Global Problems: an Examination of the Options,* we find the Trilateral view of cooperation with Communist countries.

The objective for making the report was prompted "by a desire to exploit any opportunities with the Communist countries for cooperative management of certain international problems".[13] The report did not have the objective of finding if such "cooperative management" would be advantageous to the United States or if it would enhance or reduce the security of the United States or whether it would lead to a more peaceful world. The objective *assumes* that "cooperative management" with Communist countries would be advantageous and beneficial to the United States.

On the questions of whether such cooperation would strengthen the Soviet Union, the report makes statements flatly inconsistent with well-documented fact. For example: "Some analysts have expressed concern about the consequences that are likely to flow from successful East-West collaboration in strengthening the economic capacity and therefore the international power of the Soviet Union."[14]

To which question the report answers, "These consequences are likely to be limited."[15]

ESTABLISHMENT COVER UP

Today the massive contribution of the Eastern Establishment to Soviet military development is widely known. It can no longer be suppressed as it was in the early 1970's.

Since previously "well-kept secrets" have leaked out, the new tactic is to mislead the American public into believing that it was an innocent mistake on the part of Washington policy makers. Specifically, when Jim Gallagher in the *Chicago Tribune* cites the Bryant Grinder case (precision ball bearing grinding machines were supplied to the Soviets and these machines assisted and enabled Soviet development of a family of MIRV nuclear missles with multiple war heads) and cases where electronic equipment was converted for use in missile guidance systems he says, "In both of these cases the Soviets were able to overcome serious gaps in technology with the inadvertent assistance of the United States."[16]

"Inadvertent," indeed! Many credible and acknowledged experts were vocal in the early 1970's concerning these precise shipments and identified the exact military end uses. At the Republican Convention in Miami Beach (1972) the co-author (Sutton) explained at length how such shipments would be used by the Soviets. The shipments were not inadvertent: they were deliberate and made with the full forewarning of military end uses. In the past, warnings of the possible consequences of U.S. technological aid to the Soviets have fallen on "tuned-out" ears. As the criticism became more adamant, specific attempts were made to silence it.

So we can conclude:

1. The military build-up the Soviet Union by *some* "American" multinationals through technological transfers goes back 60 years, and today is centered in the Trilaterally represented companies.

2. The blame lies almost entirely with a few international banks and big business interests. Most important among them are Chase National (now Chase Manhattan) and the **Rockefeller**-influenced General Electric and RCA complexes.

3. Warnings of the expansion of the capabilities of the Soviet military inevitably resulting from American technological aid have either been ignored, suppressed or those daring to criticize have been vilified.

4. These elitist interests are the prime source of virtually

every major crisis facing the United States today. Their greed and shortsightedness has placed the United States in the most precarious position in its entire history.

DAVID ROCKEFELLER AND SOVIET MILITARY POWER

There is no question that Trilaterals — **David Rockefeller** included — have been stung by repeated strong and widespread criticism of the Trilateral Commission.

At a 1980 World Affairs Council luncheon in Los Angeles, **Rockefeller** voiced concern that "Misrepresenting the motives of good and dedicated people will only narrow instead of broaden participation in the group's discussion of international affairs."[17]

Rockefeller specifically and at length denied that Trilateral multinationals deal with the Soviet Union for "the sake of financial gain." The *Wall Street Journal* excerpts from the Los Angeles speech boxed this **Rockefeller** comment to emphasize its importance:

> *"To some extremists, the Trilateral Commission is pictured as a nefarious plot by an Eastern Establishment of businessmen in the service of multinational corporations who will do almost anything including going into cahoots with the Kremlin for the sake of financial gain."*[18]

These are strong words. The use of buzz words such as "extremists" and "nefarious" suggests an attempt is under way to cover facts with diversionary tactics.

The weak position of Trilaterals in general is reflected in their treatment of objective, factual criticism. The usual Trilateral response to *any* criticism, whether valid or not, is to label it "extremism." The critic is immediately tagged either "far right" or "far left" or, if the facts are too accurate for comfort, the critic is merely ignored.

David Rockefeller argued further:

> *"Far from being a coterie of international conspirators with designs on covertly ruling the world, the Tri-*

lateral Commission — like the Los Angeles World Affair Council — is, in reality, a group of concerned citizens interested in fostering greater understanding and cooperation among international allies."[19]

Examine the facts above and compare them to the **Rockefeller** rhetoric. The co-author (Sutton) has written five books since 1968 on the build-up of the Soviet Union by Western capitalists. Three of the books are academic in nature, published by the Hoover Institution at Stanford University. No one, including **David Rockefeller** and **David Packard,** has denied the factual basis of these books. The Soviets have also remained silent. They know the facts are accurate. Moreover, Commissioner **David Packard,** a Trustee of the Hoover Institution, is well aware of the Stanford books. Hoover Institution financed part of the research and in the early 1970's **Packard** was personally involved with suppressing those parts that dealt with the build-up of Soviet military power.

FOOTNOTES CHAPTER 4

1. British War Cabinet Papers, 24/49/7197 Secret, April 24, 1918.

2. Ibid.

3. Antony Suttton, *Western Technology and Soviet Economic Development 1917 to 1930,* p. 290.

4. *Soviet Union Vital Goods Still Flow Despite Carter's Curbs,* Business Week, April 28, 1980, p. 42.

5. Ibid.

6. W.A. Johnson, *Daily News Digest,* July 4, 1980.

7. Antony Sutton and Patrick Wood, *Influence of the Trilateral Commission— Part I,* Trilateral Observer, Vol. 2 No. 3 (March 1979), p. 20. Trilateral Observer, P.O. Box 582, Scottsdale, Az. 85252.

8. *Nomination of Nelson A. Rockefeller of New York To Be Vice President of the United States,* Hearings before the Committee on Rules and Administration of the United States Senate. 93rd Congress 2nd Session September 23, 1974), p. 883.

9. Jack Anderson, U.P., February 8, 1980.

10. Ibid.

11. Ibid.

12. Ibid.

13. Chihiro Hosoya et al, *Collaboration with Communist Countries in Managing Global Problems,* p. 1.

14. Ibid.

15. Ibid.

16. Jim Gallagher, *Bryant Grinder Case,* Chicago Tribune, April 6, 1980.

17. *Letters to the Editor,* Wall Street Journal (April 30, 1980).

18. Ibid.

19. Ibid.

CHAPTER FIVE

ELITIST FRIENDS OF TRILATERALISM

We have previously discussed the power and membership of the Trilateral Commission, and we now need to discuss the use of this power and the influence of the Commission in a broader framework of associated elitist institutions. The Trilateral Commission does not exist in a political vacuum, it co-exists with a group of organizations which have, since about 1920, effectively taken over political power in the United States, dominated domestic and foreign policy and presently appears to be totally unrepresentative of American society as a whole.

In addition to the influence of the Trilateral Commission we have:

The Council on Foreign Relations
The Foreign Policy Association
The Atlantic Council
The Commission on Critical Choices for Americans

Together with think tanks such as Brookings Institute and Hoover Institution, these organizations constitute the source of foreign and domestic policy making in the United States. This is where ideas are generated, policies discussed, and subsequent reports written. Ideas, policies and reports are subsequently considered and discussed by all interested members of the above organizations and sooner or later a large proportion of the proposals find their way into executive decisions and/or Congressional legislation.

The overriding characteristic of this procedure is one of intellectual closed-mindedness — intellectual incest might be the best way to describe these policy creating "backwaters."

The dismal failure to create a prosperous and peaceful world during the decades-long era of American supremacy is obvious.

The Council on Foreign Relations

Founded after World War I, the Council on Foreign Relations (CFR) has been for fifty years the undisputed creator of American foreign policy.

As far back as 1959 the CFR was explicit about a need for world government:

"The U.S. must strive to build a new international order . . . including states labeling themselves as 'socialist' . . . to maintain and gradually increase the authority of the United Nations."[1]

The site for UN headquarters in New York was donated by John D. Rockefeller, Sr., and the CFR world architects for many years tried to use the United Nations as a means to develop an image of world order. Recently the focus of world order action has shifted to the Trilateral Commission, and CFR members have complained they have lost power and prestige. *"We don't have the cutting edge we once had. We're not really in the center of things,"* stated one CFR member.[2]

The problem with the CFR is that it became too large and too diverse to act as a "cutting edge" in policy creation. With several thousand members and an internal policy of bringing in membership from a diverse geographical and racial standpoint, the CFR lost its foreign affairs expertise and prestige. Today the political action has moved from the CFR to the Trilateral Commission, as aptly described by *Newsweek:*

"Since the end of World War II, U.S. foreign policy has been dominated largely by the circle of influential

men who belong to New York's Council on Foreign Relations. From Franklin D. Roosevelt to Jimmy Carter, every President has recruited council luminaries — its membership roll is a sort of Who's Who of the Eastern Establishment elite — for high level diplomatic trouble-shooting missions or for top jobs in his Administration. But the council is not universally admired. Some outsiders view it as a kind of shadow government; others dismiss it as a private club where aging foreign-policy mandarins pontificate over tea and cookies. Both views are exaggerated, but of late even some of the council's elders have grown alarmed by a sense of their organization's waning influence. The result has been a genteel furor within the book-lined confines of the council's four-story headquarters on Park Avenue."[3]

THE FOREIGN POLICY ASSOCIATION

Founded in 1918 a little before the CFR, the Foreign Policy Association (FPA) is a tax exempt educational organization supposedly to inform citizens on "challenges and problems of the United States foreign policy."[4] The FPA is purely an elitist organization. Out of fifty-six board members no fewer than twenty-nine (fifty-two percent) are members of the Council on Foreign Relations.

However, only one FPA member, **Robert R. Bowie,** is a Trilateral Commissioner, so the interlock with Trilateralism is minor.[5]

THE ATLANTIC COUNCIL OF THE UNITED STATES

The board of directors of the Atlantic Institute is comprised as follows:

Chairman: Kenneth Rush, former Deputy Secretary of State and Ambassador to France and Germany.

Vice Chairman: Henry H. Fowler, partner, Goldman Sachs & Co. and former Secretary of the Treasury.

W. Randolph Burgess, former Under Secretary of the Treasury and Ambassador to NATO and the OEEC.

Theodore C. Achilles, former Counselor of the State Department and Ambassador to Peru.

Harlan Cleveland, director, Aspen Program in International Affairs, and former Ambassador to NATO.

Emilio G. Collado, former executive vice-president, Exxon Corporation and executive director, World Bank.

Andrew J. Goodpastor, former Supreme Allied Commander Europe.

Wm. McChesney Martin, former chairman, Board of Governors, Federal Reserve System.

David Packard, chairman, Hewlett-Packard Company, and former Deputy Secretary of Defense.

Eugene V. Rostow, professor of law, Yale University, and former Under Secretary of State.

The chairman of the Atlantic Council, Kenneth Rush, was formerly of Union Carbide Corporation. He is remembered for his actively vocal role in aiding transfer of technology with military capabilities to the Soviet Union. Union Carbide is part of the "revolving door" between Washington and the New York elite.

A vice-chairman of the Atlantic Council is **David Packard**, a prominent supporter of subsidization of the Soviet Union.

A comparison of the general directors of the Atlantic Council (not on the board) compared to the Trilateral Commission is significant.

The following 11 Atlantic Council directors are also Trilateral Commissioners.

David Packard	vice-chairman of Atlantic Council
David M. Abshire	director of Atlantic Council
Anne Armstrong	former US Ambassador
Sol C. Chaikin	trade unionist
George Franklin, Jr.	coordinator of Trilateral Commission

Thomas L. Hughes	president, Carnegie Endowment
Henry A. Kissinger	executive board of Trilateral Commission
Winston Lord	chairman of the Council on Foreign Relations
Charles W. Robinson	Under Secretary of State
Robert V. Roosa	Brown Brothers, Harriman
Philip H. Trezise	former Assistant Secretary of State
Marina v.N. Whitman	vice-president of General Motors

Also,

George Ball is an honorary director of The Atlantic Council.

What are the objectives of the Atlantic Council? In its own words:

"The Atlantic Council, established seventeen years ago, seeks to promote closer mutually advantageous ties between Western Europe, North America, Japan, Australia and New Zealand. The objective is greater security and more effective harmonization of economic, monetary, energy and resource policies for the benefit of the individual in his personal, business, financial and other relations across national boundaries."[6]

Then comes a key phrase:

"In an increasingly interdependent world where 'foreign' policy is ever more closely intertwined with 'domestic' policies there is a clear need for both official and private consideration of means of dealing with problems which transcend national frontiers."[7]

Note the assumption of an "increasingly interdependent world." By placing "foreign" and "domestic" in quotes, Atlanticists are clearing the way to destroy the distinction between foreign and domestic policies, a vital step in the road to a unified world under elitist control.[8]

THE COMMISSION ON CRITICAL CHOICES FOR AMERICANS

In its own words,

> *"The Commission on Critical Choices for Americans is a nationally representative, bipartisan group of 42 prominent Americans, brought together under the chairmanship of Nelson A. Rockefeller. Their assignment: To identify the critical choices which will confront America as it embarks on its third century as a nation and to determine the realistic and desirable objectives this nation can achieve by 1985 and the year 2000.*

> *"Because of the complexity and interdependence of issues facing the world today, the Commission organized its work into six study panels, which emphasize the interrelationships of the critical choices rather than studying each one separately.*

> *"The six study panels are:*

> *Panel I -- Energy and Its Relationship to Ecology: Economics and World Stability.*

> *Panel II -- Food, Health, World Population and Quality of Life.*

> *Panel III -- Raw Materials, Industrial Development, Capital Formation, Employment and World Trade.*

> *Panel IV -- International Trade and Monetary Systems, Inflation and the Relationships Among Differing Economics Systems.*

> *Panel V -- Change, National Security and Peace, and Panel VI -- Quality of Life of Individuals and Communities in the U.S.A."*[9]

In brief, the Commission is a Rockefeller study group funded by a Rockefeller organization:

> *"The Third Century Corporation, a New York not-for-profit organization, was created to finance the work of the Commission. Since the start of its activities in the fall of 1973, the Corporation has received contributions and pledges from individuals and from foundations*

well-known for their support of public interest activities."[10]

The membership of the Commission reflects this Rockefeller influence:

MEMBERS OF THE COMMISSION ON CRITICAL CHOICES FOR AMERICANS

Chairman - Nelson E. Rockefeller
Executive Director — Henry L. Diamond

Members Ex-Officio
- Gerald R. Ford
- **Henry A. Kissinger**
- George P. Shultz
- Mike Mansfield
- Hugh Scott
- Thomas P. O'Neill, Jr.
- John J. Rhodes

Members
- Ivan Allen, Jr.
- Martin Anderson
- Robert O. Anderson
- William O. Baker
- Daniel J. Boorstin
- Norman E. Borlaug
- Ernest L. Boyer
- Guido Calabresi
- John S. Foster, Jr.
- Luther H. Foster
- Nancy Hanks Kissinger
- Belton Kleberg Johnson
- Clarence B. Jones
- **Joseph Lane Kirkland**
- John H. Knowles, M.D.
- David S. Landes
- Mary Wells Lawrence
- **Sol M. Linowitz**
- Edward J. Logue
- Clare Boothe Luce
- **Paul W. McCracken**

- Daniel Patrick Moynihan
- Bess Myerson
- William S. Paley
- Russell W. Peterson
- Wilson Riles
- Laurance S. Rockefeller
- William J. Ronan
- Oscar M. Ruebhausen
- Joseph C. Swidler
- Edward Teller
- **Marina v.N. Whitman**
- Carroll L. Wilson
- George D. Woods

Of the above members an unusual number received personal gifts from Nelson Rockefeller and were consequently under some obligation to the Rockefeller family. We know of the following cases:[11]

Henry A. Kissinger. Received a $50,000.00 gift in January 1969.

Nancy Hanks. Later married to **Henry A. Kissinger.**

Edwin J. Logue. In 1968 received a gift of $31,389 followed by another $145,000 of which $45,000 was repaid.

William J. Ronan. Received a gift of $75,000 in 1958 and $550,000 in 1974.

Henry L. Diamond. Executive Director of the Commission, received a gift of $100,000 in December 1973.

ELITIST CONTROL OF U.S. POLICY MAKING

To identify precisely elitist control over independent policy research organizations, we compared the membership of the Atlantic Council, the Council on Foreign Relations, the Trilateral Commission and the Commission on Critical Choices for Americans to find out how many members of one organization served with other organizations. (the Foreign Policy Association appears to be a special case which we will note only briefly.)

We grouped the interlocks into three categories: *Quadruple, Triple* and *Double Hats* — depending upon his/her membership in these organizations.

QUADRUPLE HATS

The Rockefeller family is represented directly in all four organizations, and also indirectly, as will be discussed later.

David Rockefeller is chairman of both the Trilateral Commission and the Council on Foreign Relations. The late Nelson Rockefeller was an honorary director of the Atlantic Council and created the Commission on Critical Choices for Americans. In addition, Laurance Rockefeller served on the Commission on Critical Choices.

In brief, there is direct, at-the-top Rockefeller family participation in all four organizations. Logically, these organizations do not reflect American society as a whole, but presumably those interests represented by the Rockefeller family — whatever those interests might be.

This extraordinary influence cannot be denied except by some intellectually dishonest mind "blank." Those researchers and journalists who choose to ignore this unparalleled influence over domestic and foreign policy making need to reconsider their basic moral position.

Without doubt, the influence of the Rockefeller family on US policy making is now and has been for many decades a topic demanding urgent and thorough investigation.

Apart from the Rockefeller family, the most notable "quadruple hat" is that of **Henry Kissinger.** Let's briefly look at the **Kissinger-Rockefeller** ties:

- In 1955, **Kissinger,** then an obscure Harvard professor, was chosen to head the Rockefeller Brothers Fund. Objective? To develop studies to formulate American foreign policy for the 1960's. An ambitious and farsighted project; however, we are unable to determine what constitutional or moral sanction gave the Rockefeller family the right to determine US policy.

- Nelson Rockefeller has described **Kissinger** as a "close personal friend and associate for more than eighteen years." (1974).

- In January 1969, **Kissinger** resigned as a personal foreign policy consultant to Nelson Rockefeller and became assistant to President Nixon for national security affairs. Nelson Rockefeller presented

Kissinger with a gift of $50,000 at that time. The gift was made in Rockefeller's own words as a token of "my affection and appreciation."

- The amount paid by Nelson Rockefeller to **Kissinger** over the period 1958 to 1968 is a matter of public record. These amounts are not unsubstantial:

1958	$ 3,000
1959	7,000
1960	12,000
1961	12,000
1962	12,000
1963	14,000
1964	18,000
1965	11,250
1966	9,000
1967	15,500
1968	28,000
1969	50,000

(The last gift was on joining President Nixon.)

The official report notes that these payments were for work "done for the family rather than on a consulting basis through any governmental agency."[12]

In summary, quadruple hat **Kissinger** can without prejudice be described as a hired intellectual servant of the Rockefeller family.

TRIPLE HATS

When we come to look at triple hats, we notice at least two interesting facts: 1) There are seven triple hats, compared to only three quadruple hats and 2) with minor exceptions, these triple hats have a Rockefeller or international banking association.

The triple hats that sit on the Trilateral Commission, Council on Foreign Relations and the Atlantic Council include: **George S. Franklin, Winston Lord, Robert Roosa, George Ball, Thomas L. Hughes, Charles W. Robinson** and **Philip Trezise.**

George S. Franklin was formerly coordinator of the Atlantic

Council, executive director of the Council on Foreign Relations and is presently coordinator of the Trilateral Commission. Thus, in one pair of hands, there is concentrated the executive power, wielded by the secretary of a committee of three policy-making organizations. Since the Committee on Critical Choices was a temporary organization, there was no coordinating required and presumably no requirement for **George Franklin's** talents.

Winston Lord is president of the Council on Foreign Relations (**David Rockefeller** is chairman), a director of the Atlantic Council and a Trilateral Commissioner.

Robert Roosa is a trustee of the Rockefeller Foundation and shuttles between a partnership in Brown Brothers, Harriman (Harriman is prominent in the military buildup of the Soviet Union through US technology) and subcabinet posts in Washington.

George Ball is a partner in another international Wall Street banking firm — Lehman Brothers — and a long time shuttler between Washington political and banking circles.

The remaining triple hat is **Marina v. Neumann Whitman,** a former professor of economics at the University of Pittsburgh and recently a vice president at General Motors.

Apart from virtually unknown **Whitman,** the **Rockefeller** interests are the *only* individual interests represented on all four policy-making bodies.

We might ask how the impressive investigative powers of *The Washington Post* and the *New York Times* managed to miss such an obvious conflict of interest; or, for that matter, we might ask the same question about the *Conservative Digest.*

DOUBLE HATS

When we get to double hats, the extraordinary overlap among these organizations is identified. No less than sixty-five percent of the directors of the Atlantic Council are also members of the CFR including its chairman Kenneth Rush — a key supporter of aid to the Soviet Union — and all seven vice presidents except for **David Packard,** who is a double hat on the

Trilateral Commission and CFR.)

Out of eighty-two directors of the Atlantic Council, no fewer than fifty-three members of the CFR and out of twenty-four honorary directors, fourteen are also members of the CFR. That gives us a total of seventy-four members out of a total of one hundred fourteen Atlantic Council directors.

		COUNCIL ON FOREIGN RELATIONS		
NAME OF MEMBER	ATLANTIC COUNCIL	FOREIGN RELATIONS	TRILATERAL COMMISSION	COMMISSION ON CRITICAL CHOICES
David Abshire	X		X	
Anne Armstrong	X		X	
George Ball	X	X	X	
Sol C. Chaikin	X		X	
George S. Franklin	X	X	X	
Thomas L. Hughes	X	X	X	
Henry Kissinger	X	X	X	X
Winston Lord	X	X	X	
David Packard	X		X	
Charles W. Robinson	X	X	X	
Nelson Rockefeller	X	X		X
Robert Roosa	X	X	X	
Philip H. Trezise	X	X	X	
Marina v.N. Whitman	X	X	X	X

The interlock that will interest most readers is that between the traditional elitist foreign policy base (CFR) and the newer elitist vehicle, the Trilateral Commission. The authors compared the 1977-78 CRF and the 1978 Trilateral Commission membership lists.

The highlights of the interlock are as follows:

- Out of ninety-one North American Trilateral Commissioners, forty-eight (fifty-three percent) are members of the CFR. (Remember this also includes Canadian Commissioners, so the purely US figure is closer to sixty percent.)
- When we come to the category "Former Members in Public Service," the percentage is almost unbelievable. Of eighteen Commissioners who served in Washington

in the Carter administration, fifteen were members of the CFR — This is eighty-three per cent!

The three Trilateral Commissioners *not* members of CFR but who were in Washington are **Jimmy Carter, Walter Mondale** and **Lucy Wilson Benson,** who later became US Under Secretary of State.

In conclusion, we can readily see the tremendous overlap in membership and control of these important policy-making organizations.

FOOTNOTES CHAPTER 5

1. Study No. Seven, quoted in *Organization #11,* Network of Patriotic Letter writers.

2. New York Times, November 21, 1971, p. 2 col. 1.

3. Angus Deming and Tony Fuller, *Foreign Policy: Mandarins in Trouble,* Newsweek, March 28, 1977.

4. Whitney H. Shepardson, *Early History of the Council on Foreign Relations,* p. 8.

5. See information contained in footnote number 8.

6. Ibid.

7. Ibid.

8. For further information, contact The Atlantic Council of the United States, 1616 H Street, NW, Washington, DC 20006 and *Report on the Foreign Policy Association* published by Doorstep Savannah, 409 East Liberty Street, Savannah, Georgia. Enclose $1.00.

9. Helen Kitchen, *Africa: From Mystery To Maze,* Critical Choices for Americans, Volume XI, pp v-vi.

10. Ibid.

11. Ibid.

CHAPTER SIX:

TRILATERAL FOREIGN POLICY AND HUMAN RIGHTS

THE CASE OF COMMUNIST CHINA

Trilateral foreign policy as it was implemented in the **Carter** administration appeared to be intent on donating American assets and enterprises to the Marxist world as rapidly as public awareness will allow. This observation is not limited to this author. In fact, Vermont Royster writing in *The Wall Street Journal* made a new high for that publication, which is normally subservient to Trilateral ambitions; Royster commented on the new **Carter** agreement with Communist China:

> "The Carter administration has agreed to normaliza-
> tion of relations with the People's Republic — i.e., full
> diplomatic recognition — on terms no different from
> those the Chinese would have welcomed at any time
> since 1972.

> "Moreover, we suddenly accepted the Chinese terms,
> previously rejected by Presidents Nixon and Ford, not
> because of any new necessity for the U.S. to normalize
> those relations at this time. The U.S. could have

continued the existing relationship, awkward though it was, almost indefinitely without any injury to our national interests.

"Instead we simply accepted every condition the People's Republic has demanded all along, including a formal acceptance by us, without any qualification, of the People's Republic claim that Taiwan is an integral part of Mainland China."[1]

In short, we have one more example of the American proclivity to think that reaching an agreement is somehow more important than what's in the agreement.

Moreover, this inclination toward giving everything away is seen by Trilaterals as an imperative. Witness **Zbigniew Brzezinski** writing at the time of the Communist China debacle:

"And, last but not least, we have to accomodate very broadly with the People's Republic of China. It represents one-fourth of humanity, and as extremely gifted and creative segment of humanity, with whom we have many common interests. These interests are long-term, not tactically anti-Soviet; they are much more connected with our fundamental view of a world of diversity and not a world dominated by this or that power."[2]

THE U.S. — COMMUNIST CHINA AGREEMENT

The Carter administration agreement with Communist China, the so-called normalization of relations, was an extraordinary treaty. All the Chinese terms, including those rejected by Presidents Nixon and Ford, were totally accepted in the Trilateral negotiations (the negotiators were all Trilaterals). On the spot in Peking was **Leonard Woodcock.** In Washington were **Cyrus Vance** and **Warren Christopher** (Under Secretary of State for East Asian and Pacific Affairs.)

There was no pressure to make an agreement at this time from the strategic or political viewpoint — so we must look to the multinationals for an answer. What do they gain? Is the China treaty a duplicate of the early 1920-30 Soviet agreement? A device to fill multinational order books and expand the loan base of international banks?

The United States was in an extremely strong bargaining position. The Chinese need US technology to survive and US credits to buy technology. They need the US as an ally against Russian intrusions over the Chinese border and recognition by the US gives the Chinese Communists a status they can achieve in no other way.

Yet the United States capitulated without a whimper, very much like the Vietnamese situation when the US got sucked into a major war without plan or purpose where some 50,000 Americans were killed. The battlefield was abandoned at a time when America still had the absolute capability to finish the military job. In other words, we apparently did not know why we were in Vietnam in the first place. When we *were* involved, we spent billions on war materials and even then lacked the will to use those weapons.

In this instance and others we can find a common thread, a common explanation. In science, the answer that most likey is true, is that answer which fits the largest number of cases or events. Is there profit for Wall Street in recognizing Communist China? Was there also profit in $300 billion of Vietnamese military contracts? In the same way, there was profit in saving the Soviets and building the Soviet Five-Year Plans in the 1930's.

This is the simplest, most plausible answer. It fits the greatest number of cases — and this is where Trilateralism comes in. Trilateralism is the vehicle by which *some* banking interests and multinationals carry out their policy objectives.

The Trilateral opening to Communist China also reveals a total failure to recognize the human cost of Chinese Communism: 200 million Chinese dead in the thirty years of the Revolution. During one particular campaign, *Let a Million Flowers Bloom,* Chinese Communists lifted their restrictions on freedom of speech and action. Many Chinese then took the bait to criticize the regime. After a few months of freedom of speech the Chinese government promptly arrested the dissidents and used their own words as evidence to send them to labor camps, prisons, or to their death.

Internationalist businessmen are adept at telling each other how non-political and smart they are to ignore civil and social conditions while concentrating on the business at hand. The profit statement is the guide: hard-core amorality.

The dangerous illusions Trilaterals hold about Russia and China do not therefore stem from ignorance of the facts — their actions stem from extreme shortsightedness and amorality. An upcoming contract for a multinational corporation has total precedence over any nonsense about human rights. While, for example, Trilateral **J.Paul Austin**[3] may want to sell Coca-Cola to 800 million Chinese, **Austin** seems to have little interest in what happened to tens of millions of the less fortunate Chinese.

The outright betrayal of Taiwan in the clear, stark words of the official agreement reads as follows:

> *"The government of the United States of America acknowledges the Chinese position that there is but one China, and Taiwan is part of China."*[4]

It is difficult to find any historical parallel where a country has acknowledged the slaughter of 200 million people by creating an alliance with that country. Possibly the closest parallel is Hitler's alliance with Stalin in 1939 after Stalin had murdered millions of peasants and Hitler had begun to move against his enemies.

For Trilaterals, human rights are subordinate to their objective of world control. Witness the following statement:

> *". . . the support for human rights will have to be balanced against other important goals of world order. Some Trilateral conceptions of detente with the Soviet Union and other communist states tend to conflict with a policy promoting human rights."*[5]

The drive to open up Communist China as a captive market for globalist corporations has its parallel in the early days of the Soviet Union.

THE HISTORICAL PARALLEL

Many of the same companies now in China (some have since changed their names or merged with other companies) were equally responsible for rescuing the infant and collapsing Soviet Russia in 1922. In the early 1920's the Soviet Union was on the verge of collapse. The only industrial structure was that of the Czars. Industry was dormant, not destroyed as Soviet propagandists would have us believe. Foreign firms, mainly American and German, came in to start up the sleeping Czarist industry and remained to build the Five-Year Plans. Why? Because the Soviets had killed or dispersed the skilled engineers and managers needed to run industry. As Soviet Commissar Krassif phrased the problem:

> *"Anyone can help pull down a house; there are but a few who can rebuild. In Russia there happened to be far fewer than anywhere else."[6]*

Communist China today is in the same situation as Soviet Russia in the 1920's. To quote a recent statement by Chaing Ching-Kuo of Taiwan:

> *"The Chinese Communists are on the verge of collapse at this moment. The United States's establishment of relations with the Communist is to help save a bandit regime that massacres millions and millions of compatriots. Therefore, America is the biggest sinner in history."[7]*

The same multinationals that built the Soviet Union into a vast military power are now doing the same with Communist China. China suffers from widespread electricity shortages and has had to buy Westinghouse-engineered nuclear reactors from France. The iron and steel industry is backward and inefficient. Planned increases are based on use of Western technology, as were the Soviets' in the early 1920's and 1930's. The following table illustrates how American firms involved in the USSR — even before establishment of diplomatic relations — have also been negotiating with Communist China, and in some cases, like Coca-Cola, well before the establishment of diplomatic relations.

	SOVIET RUSSIA 1920-1930	COMMUNIST CHINA 1978
Ingersoll-Rand	Represented by Armand Hammer from about 1918 onwards.	Dec. 1978 order for 2 large water well drills for $1 million
Boeing Aircraft	Technical assistance	Sales of 4 jumbo jets 747-SP
Universal Oil Products	1938 contract for hydrogenation and iso-octane plants.	Petrochemical plants

Take the example of Boeing Aircraft (**T.A. Wilson** is chairman of the board). In the 1930's Boeing supplied technical assistance to the growing Soviets. The Soviet I-16 fighter was patterned on the Boeing P-26. The Soviet TU-4 four-engine bomber was a copy of the Boeing B-29 and could only have been reproduced with US assistance. Boeing is now selling to Communist China.

Another example is UOP (Universal Oil Products), now a subsidiary of Signal Oil Company. In the 1930s UOP had contracts in the USSR for construction of hydrogenation plants, which were of vital importance for military purposes. Up to 1938 the Soviets were unable to produce 87-94 octane gasoline for aviation use. Hydrogenation plants built by UOP converted 85 octane gasoline from the Saratov and Grozny refineries into 95 octane avgas. Currently, UOP is one of the first American firms in China to develop petrochemical industry — also vital for war purposes.

Yet another example is Ingersoll-Rand which was represented in the Soviet Union by Armand Hammer (now chairman of Occidental Petroleum Corporation) as early as 1918. At that time Armand Hammer's father, Julius Hammer, was secretary of the Communist Party USA. Ingersoll-Rand became a prime seller of technology to the USSR. In 1979, Ingersoll-Rand is following the same road with Communist China.

Dozens of firms can be cited with similar stories. As previously noted, US multinationals built Soviet power. This has cost the United States hundreds of thousands of lives in Korea and Vietnam. Now these same multinationals have begun to build Communist China. The following table demonstrates the widespread fundamental nature of the early Chinese contracts. Apart from Coca-Cola, they involve advanced technology with outright military application.

Recent Western Contracts with Communist China

US Firm	Work in Communist China	Comments
Coca-Cola	Monopoly of soft drinks	Chairman **J. Paul Austin** was prime Atlanta backer of **Jimmy Carter**
Control Data	12 CDC Cyber computers	$69 million
U.S. Steel	One of the world's largest iron ore mines	Probably over $1 billion. Packard and Shepard are directors
Pullman Inc.	Petrochemical	Multimillion-
Hercules Inc.	facility	dollar
UOP		
Mitsui Petro Chemical	Four petrochemical plants	$205 million (**Ikeda** is a Trilateral)
Boeing Aircraft	Three 747-SP Jumbos	$156 million (**Wilson** and **Weyerhaeuser** are directors)
LTV Corp.	Oil drilling equipment	$40 million

THE CHASE MANHATTAN BANK

Chase Manhattan was the first bank into Communist China and probably has the most to profit from its build-up. Back in the 1920's the forerunner of the Chase Manhattan Bank, Chase National Bank, was deeply involved in building the Soviets — some of this activity was called illegal and was certainly against US official policy.

Both Chase National and Equitable Trust were the leaders in the Soviet credit business at a time when the State Department had specifically banned credits to Soviet Russia. Chase evaded the ban by accepting platinum from Soviet mines and advancing credit on the basis of these shipments. Again, this was strictly against US policy in the 1920's.

The president of the American-Russian Chamber of Commerce in the 1920's was Reeve Schley, also a vice-president of Chase National. The Chamber was a pressure group which sought to change US policy into recognition of the USSR and and open up the Russian market for some major American firms and banks.To this end, the Chamber used known Communists as agents; for example, a Chamber delegation to Russia in 1936 was lead by Charles Haddell Smith, previously described by the State Department as "in the employ of the Soviets and a member of the Soviet Peasant International."[8] Members of the Chamber in the 1920's included many of the firms opening up the China trade today, including Deere & Co., Westinghouse and Chase National.

THE NEW CHINA POLICY IS A TRILATERAL POLICY

Some major important China contracts link to Trilateralists and their corporate affiliates are:

- The key financial backer of **Jimmy Carter** was Coca-Cola chairman and Trilateral Commissioner **J. Paul Austin,** Coca-Cola will have a soft drink monopoly in China. Maybe the Chinese don't yet know what a soft drink tastes like, but 800 million Chinese are prime market for the 21st century. Coca-Cola has been negotiating for ten years with the Chinese, i.e. long before any public surfacing of a "new" China policy and presumably while the Chinese aided the killing of Americans in Vietnam.
- A consortium of US oil companies in negotiating development of Chinese petroleum resources. These include Exxon (**David Rockefeller** has dominant interests), Pennzoil, Phillips and Union Oil.
- Time magazine Man-of-the-Year was the Chinese Communist leader, Teng Hsiao-Ping. Trilateralist **Hedley Donovan** was editor-in-chief of Time.
- The first American banks into China were Chase Manhattan and the First National Bank of Chicago.
- Japanese Trilaterals are heavily involved in construction of Communist China — as described below.

Trilateral policy on Communist China has been spelled out

clearly. Trilateral-Chinese cooperation has been proposed in the following areas, but not limited to them:

1. Earthquake warning
2. Energy: Above all, it is emphasized that China's oil potential can only be exploited by developing the off-shore reserves on the continental shelf. "This would probably require outside technology. US oil companies have shown interest in investing in continental shelf oil exploration."[9]

In brief, Trilateral publications outlined the **Carter** administration policies were later and still are being followed.

JAPANESE TRILATERALS AND CHINA

Japanese members of the Trilateral Commission reflect the Japanese establishment to an extraordinary degree. This is significant because Japan is now in the forefront of building Communist China.

The breakdown of Japanese Trilaterals is as follows:

	Trilateral Commissioners	*Executive Committee*
Business	37	1
Banks	14	3
Education	13	2
Government	5	3
Media	2	0
Unions	2	0

The previous chairman of the Japanese Trilateral Executive Committee is **Chujiro Funjino,** chairman of the Mitsubishi Corporation. Mitsubishi has contracts in China including a large contract to modernize the Shanghai shipyards, the largest in Communist China.

Three Japanese banks are represented on the Executive Committee of the Trilateral Commission: The president of the Bank of Tokyo, **Yusuka Kashiwagi** is a former special advisor to the Minister of Finance, **Saburo Okita** is president of the Overseas Economic Cooperation Fund, and **Takeshi Watanabe** is chairman of Trident International Finance, Ltd., based in Hong Kong.

Former Japanese government officials comprise more than one-third of the executive committee: **Kiichi Miyazawa** is a Minister of State and Chinese Cabinet Secretary, **Ryuji Takeuchi** is advisor to the Minister for Foreign Affairs and a former ambassador to the United States and **Nobuhiko Ushiba** is also a former ambassador to the United States. Japanese trade unions have two representatives, **Kazuo Oikawa,** who is president of the Japan Telecommunications workers union and **Ichiro Shioji,** president of the Confederation of Japan Automobile workers union.

The opening up of Communist China is a vital Trilateral policy and Japanese Trilaterals are in the forefront of the rush for contracts:

- **Yoshizo Ikeda** is president of Mitsui & Co., which has numerous Chinese contracts. Mitsui Petrochemical Industries Ltd. is involved in construction of polyethylene plants.
- **Seiki Tozaki** is president of Itoh & Co., which is involved in trading contracts with Communist China.
- **Hirokichi Yoshiyama** is president of Hitachi Ltd. His firm has a $100 million contract to supply equipment for the Paoshan steelworks and will expand the Hungchi Shipyards at Luta.
- **Yoshihiro Inayama** is chairman of Nippon Steel which is also aiding development of the Communist steel industry, including a $3 billion steel plant just outside Shanghai.

In brief:
1. The current China policy is Trilateral policy.
2. The 1978 agreement was complete capitulation to Chinese Communist terms.
3. The only rational explanation for capitulation is that the power elite is focusing more on the contracts to be won than on the long-run strategic impact on our world.

THE CASE OF THE PANAMA CANAL

The Panama Canal Treaty handed over US property, bought and full payment made, many decades ago. The zone was under US sovereignty but handed over to a Marxist (Torrijos) regime.

Some 76% of America disapproved of the Panama treaties. Those Americans who supported the Treaties are usually described as either liberals who believe Panama is a "have not" nation more deserving of the Canal Zone or those who wish to ignore the fact of legal US ownership, although this ownership has been precisely documented to Congress.

In 1977, Congressman Robert K. Dornan identified a third group of treaty supporters — what Dornan called "the fast-money type of international banker." Dornan demonstrated that the Panama overseas debt required 39% of the Panamanian gross national product. Further, the Torrijos government was far from stable and the banks participating in this debt wanted to protect their investment. Consequently, the Panama Canal treaties gave Torrijos a much needed boost to keep his Marxist regime in power and keep the bank debt from default.

Here is an excerpt from Congressman Dornan's report to Congress:

> *"The most visible and known of this third type are the fast-money type of international banker. The Torrijos dictatorship is up to its ears in debt to banks. The debt of the Torrijos regime has now reached such proportions that 39 percent of the Panama GNP — repeat 39 percent — goes to debt servicing alone. This might not cause the extreme consternation in the banking circles that it does if it were a debt owed by a stable government. But the Torrijos regime is far from stable. The dictator was nearly ousted a few years ago by an abortive coup and there are few wagers on his staying in power long if the treaties are rejected by the Senate. And if he is not in power, the banks do not have much chance of getting their money.*

> *"Some Members of Congress and Americans are*

aware of the conflict of interests involved in some of the banks' support of the Panamanian treaties. They are aware of the marine Midland connection through negotiator Sol Linowitz. But there are many other banks whose endorsement of the giveaway of the canal may be motivated by monetary interests. Unlike Marine Midland, they have been able to keep a lower profile. They are not generally known to be part of the banking group with a lucrative stake in the ratification of the treaties."[10]

Dornan published a list of banks participating in the Torrijos debt and also pointed out that **Sol Linowitz,** the US negotiator, was a director of Marine Midland Bank that held part of two Panamaniam loans — thus establishing clear conflict of interest for **Linowitz.**

The authors examined the list of banks (thirty-one for one loan and fourteen for another loan) publicized by Congressman Dornan and traced the Trilateral links to these participating banks. The results are truly astounding. There are only three hundred Trilateral Commissioners worldwide, of which about one-third are from Japan, one-third from Europe and one-third from the United States, i.e., about 90 from each region. For the two Panamanian loans cited by Congressman Dornan we found: (1) No fewer than thirty-two Trilaterals are on the boards of the thirty-one banks participating in the Republic of Panama $115 million 10-year Eurodollar loan issued in 1972. (2) Also, fifteen Trilaterals were on the boards of fourteen banks participating in the Republic of Panama $20 million floating rate promissory note issued in 1972. (3) These links suggest conflict of interest on a gigantic scale, involving not only the **Carter** administration but the Japanese government and less importantly some European governments.

To quote Congressman Dornan again:

"But there is a third type of protreaty person whose motives should be impugned. These persons are well aware of the facts of the 1903 treaty and the importance of the canal to the security of the Western World. They do not endorse the treaty out of undue love of the

Panamanian people or out of confusion -- they do so out of self-interest. They have something to gain from the giveaway of the American people's canal."[11]

TRILATERAL ASSUALT ON HUMAN RIGHTS

Trilateral writings on human rights is notable for its paucity. No Trilateral Task Force Report has been devoted to the basic question of individual freedoms and survival in an age of ever-increasing government. On the contrary, Trilateral writing has focused on the rights and powers of governmental authority rather than the rights of the governed.

In the arena of public discussion and political maneuvering, some rather transparent lip service is given to human rights. Trilateralists and the **Carter** administration expressed a superficial "deep concern" for human rights and they convinced many that human rights are a fundamental objective of Trilateralism. For example, as proclaimed by Trilateral **Warren Christopher,** Deputy Under Secretary of State:

"The major accomplishment of the [President's human rights] *policy is that we've helped to create a concern all around the world for basic human rights."[12]*

We have to presume that **Warren Christopher** and the State Department public relations officials kept straight faces when they released that statement. In fact, nothing could be further from the truth. A few examples demolish **Warren Christopher's** expression of concern.

PROPERTY RIGHTS SUBORDINATED

In October 1977, President **Carter** signed the Soviet version of the UN Universal Declaration of Human Rights. Seven previous Presidents had refused to sign the Declaration because it excludes *the right to own property.* Traditional American philosophy is that without property rights there can be no "human rights."

RUSSIAN CHRISTIANS AND THE US EMBASSY IN MOSCOW

For two year a group of seven Russian Christians have been isolated in the US Embassy in Moscow — the same State Department that **Warren Christopher** says has a concern for human rights. According to Associated Press:

> *"They pray, read their Bibles, beset by fears and doubts. On one side of the room a Russian barber loudly slurs them to customers and on the other side through an iron grilled window Soviet guards occasionally shout taunts."[13]*

Why are these Russian refugees slurred and taunted on US property?

Because US Embassy officials want them to return to the Soviets, even though they have already been granted political asylum. Why? Because the **Carter** administration found the presence of these Russian Christians to be embarrassing. They are kept exposed to threats and taunts to "encourage" them to return to a Soviet prison rather than refuge in the US Embassy.

Comments Rev. Blakhoslav Hruby, director of the Research Center for Religion and Human Rights in Closed Societies:

> *"It's a real scandal. . . their refuge has become a prison . . . although there are thousands of worse cases of human rights violations in the world this one is particularly shameful because these people are suffering — and for so long — in U.S. hands."[14]*

Hruby adds:

> *"The fate of these gentle, courageous, but defenseless Christians depends in a large part on how we in the West respond to their tragic predicament. There is no place for them to turn and nowhere for them to go. America is their last hope.*
>
> *"But the embassy seems more embarrassed by their presence than concerned. They're being treated as expendable in the name of so-called 'broader' diplomacy. But these are specific human lives and they*

aren't being treated like human beings.

"Every week, embassy officials advise them to go, and they're becoming terribly depressed and discouraged. Yet if they finally give up and decide to go because they're being made so miserable, they'd be sent to Siberia to die of an 'accident'."[15]

This was the situation in the US Embassy in Moscow while Trilateralists **Carter** and **Christopher** pontificted to the world about human rights. And at the beginning of the Reagan administration, those Russian Christians *still* remain in captivity!

Trilateral involvement in human rights is an exercise in double standards. Some countries are criticized, some countries are not — depending on political objectives.

The double standard on human rights necessitated by Trilateralist objectives, was vividly demonstrated in 1978 by State Department spokesman John Trattner. The administration decided to return the Crown of St. Stephen to Communist Hungary after safekeeping in the US since 1951. At a press conference, Reed Irvine of *Accuracy in Media,* Washington, D.C., pinned the administration to the wall on the double standard with dagger-like questions:

Irvine: *The State Department is very much concerned with representative government these days. They are concerned in Rhodesia and South Africa. Are you at all concerned with whether the government of Hungary is representative of the people?*

Trattner: *Our concern about representative government around the world does not also mean that we stand up here and make judgments from this podium as to the question you are asking here.*

Irvine: *I see. Could you tell us when the last free election was held in Hungary?*

Trattner: *I would have to go back and look at the history books. I don't really know.*

Irvine: *Has Janos Kadar ever submitted himself to a free election?*

Trattner: *I think what you ought to do is ask the*

Hungarians.

Irvine: *You know that. You know he hasn't.*

Trattner: *Well, then, why do you ask the question?*

Irvine: *I wanted to get the State Departments's view of why they feel that this government ...*

Trattner: *My answer is that from this podium we are not in the habit of making judgments on other people's governments however much we may have opinions about them and however much to you the answer may be obvious, or it may be obvious to you that I know what the answer is. On the record, up here, up here, I am not going to give an answer.*

Irvine: *You don't have opinions about representative governments in Rhodesia and South Africa?*

Trattner: *No, I am not saying that at all.*

Irvine: *You say you are returning the crown to the Hungarian people. You are returning it to the government, to Janos Kadar, who obviously doesn't represent the people, because he has never submitted himself to an election. Therefore you are saying, it seems to me incorrectly, that the government of Hungary represents the people, and by this action you are indicating to everyone in the world that this government has your approbation.*

Trattner: *No, I would contest that strongly. I don't think I am making that kind of statement at all.*

Irvine: *Are we getting any quid pro quo for this? Are the Hungarians doing anything — relaxing any restraints on human rights in return for this action?*

Trattner: *There are many Hungarian-Americans who have been in touch with us who have suggested that we should seek some concessions from the Hungarian government in return for the crown. Others in the Hungarian-American community have told us that because of the unique significance of the crown to all Hungarians, they feel it would be inappropriate and disrespectful to a centuries-old tradition to trade the crown for anything of that kind could possibly have an equivalent or comparible significance. We agree with the latter point of view, and recognizing that we received the crown for safekeeping without any other conditions, we stated our willingness to the Hungarian government to return it in the same manner.*

Irvine: *Could you tell us why we didn't return it much earlier then?*

Trattner: *We have always said that the return of the crown would be done in the context of an improvement in relations bilaterally, and we feel that that point has been reached.*

Irvine: *Has there been some remarkable change in the last year that would have altered . . .?*

Trattner: *Yes, I can cite you a few things . . . The overall record of Hungary in implementing the Helinsinki Final Act has been among the best in the Warsaw Pact, although its performance still falls short of Western standards.*

Irvine: *How does it compare with South Africa?*

Trattner: *I am not in the business right now, at least, of making a comparison with South Africa for you.*

Irvine: *Do they have as much freedom of the press as South Africa?*

Trattner: *I can't make a comparison for you.*

Irvine: *Do they have any freedom of the press? Are there any free newspapers in Hungary that are not run by the government?*

Trattner: *I really don't know.*

Irvine: *Could you find out?*

Trattner: *It might be possible to find out, yes.*[16]

For those readers who may not know the answers evaded by the State Department, the Hungarian press is *totally* controlled by the Hungarian government, and no opposition newspapers or publications are allowed. South Africa, on the other hand, has one of the most vocal and critical presses in the world: read a few issues of the *Rand Daily Mail* or the *Cape Times* and this point is made amply clear.

IDI AMIN AND TRILATERALISM

Remember Idi Amin, the Ugandan leader, who systematically butchered his own population?

Far from Trilateral protests over Amin's butchery we find official US government support, as reported by Jack Anderson:

> *"With great show of disapproval, the U.S. cut off Amin's foreign aid in 1973. Yet he flies around in grand style in a Grumman Gulfstream jet that is serviced every year at the company plant in Savannah. Georgia Page Airways, another American company, has provided flight crews to maintain Amin's imperial plane.*
>
> *We reported last fall that still another American company, Bell Helicopter, was training 20 police pilots at Fort Worth. They now operate at least nine Bell helicopters, which were sent unarmed to Uganda, but could easily have been converted into para-military aircraft.*
>
> *We have now learned that the 20 pilots, who hastily returned to Uganda after our report was published, were admitted to the U.S. on A-2 priority diplomatic visas. Confidential sources say 82 Ugandans entered the country on diplomatic visas. Several of them belong to Amin's notoriously brutal State Research Bureau."[17]*

What is the Trilateral comment? **Warren Christopher** merely had this observation to Anderson's revelations:

> *"A small number of Ugandan pilots are being trained by private U.S. firms."[18]*

And **Jimmy Carter** then handed out a weak-handed slap officially, while unofficially allowing the training of Ugandans to continue:

> *"We must strengthen our efforts to condemn the practices of that government."[19]*

RELEVANCE OF HUMAN RIGHTS

The Fall 1978 issue of *Trialogue*, official organ of the Trilateral Commission, was devoted to **"The Politics of Human Rights."**

A leadoff interview with Trilateral **Henry Kissinger** summarized the Trilateral use of human rights as a policy subordinate to other policies and a tool to be used to achieve overall objectives.

Kissinger expressed it this way in reply to a question:

> Q. *What are the merits and chances of successes of a vocal human rights policy on the part of the U.S. Administration* [sic]?
>
> A. *It has some merit for the United States to stand for its principles: the United States should definitely do so — and indeed, we tried to do this also in the administrations with which I was associated. However, I think that making this a vocal objective of our foreign policy involves great dangers: You run the risk of either showing your impotence or producing revolutions in friendly countries, or both . . . I think that fundamental goals of American policy, no matter how they are defined, should be linked to other elements of interest to the Soviets. Either a policy has relevance to other areas of national strategy, or it has no meaning whatsoever. Linkage, therefore, is synonymous with overall strategic view. It is inherent in the real world, and if we ignore it, it is only at our peril.*[20]

That's it in a nutshell. "Either a policy has relevance to other areas of national strategy, or it has no meaning whatsoever." In brief, human rights have no meaning for **Kissinger** and his Trilateral friends — human rights are gambling chips to be used as, and when, the elitists see fit.

SLAVES IN COLOMBIA

Trilaterals Over Washington, Volume I, detailed the links between some US multinationals and international banks with Trilateralism and argued that Trilateral objectives are no more than self-interested objectives for some MNC's and international bankers.

Stark evidence for this argument was revealed in 1975-6 by the use of "slave-labor-at-a-profit" by Trilateral multinationals in Colombia, Latin America. While the slave labor system is not widely known even among public officials in Colombia, it apparently has widespread use.

Under the Colombian system of law an accused person can be kept in prison without bail for periods which may extend up to ten years. About 6,000 such "prisoners," actually political detainees, work on "prison labor projects" run by corporations, including prominent US multinationals. As the knowledge of this forced labor surfaced, comments by both American residents and Colombian officials support the authors' argument on Trilateral human rights policy:

> *"It's especially bad for multinationals to do this in an underdeveloped country," said Fernando Umana, head of Colombia's only public interest law firm.*
>
> *Oscar A. Bradford, President of the Colombian-American Chamber of Commerce, hadn't heard of the practice until 1975. He commented at that time, "If I were a corporate executive, I'd be inclined to look for something a little less controversial. God knows there are enough other areas of social reform in which to apply corporate efforts and resources."[21]*

On June 20, 1975 the *Wall Street Journal* reported this detail:

> *"Now there are plans afoot to turn the entire prison population into 'employees' of national and multinational companies. This is a proposal of Action in Colombia, a non-profit group backed financially by 70 large Colombian and U.S. concerns ranging from Avianca, the national airline, to local units of Bank of America, Dow Chemical Co. and International Business Machines Corp. So far, an Action official says, Colombian and US businessmen have responded 'very favorably' to the plan, which is put forward as a program for rehabilitation and improvement of the prisoners' lot."[22]*

The MNC's and banks who use slave labor in Colombia while trumpeting "human rights" to an unsuspecting American public, include Trilateral members:

- Bank of America (Trilateralist **Clausen** and **Wood**)

which is backing Action in Colombia to turn "the entire prison population of Colombia into employees of national and multinational companies."[23]

- Container Corporation of America (100% owned by Mobil Oil) has operated a "slave labor" production line for many years. Container Corporation is also affiliated with Marcor Inc., another Mobil subsidiary. A Trilateralist in this group is **Robert S. Ingersoll** (First Chicago Corporation), also a trustee of the Aspen Institute for Humanistic Studies.
- Chase Manhattan owns 5.2 percent of Mobil Oil stock, and there are six Trilaterals on the Chase board.

IBM is also cited as a supporter of Action in Colombia. Trilateralists on the IBM board include **W.T. Coleman, Jr., William W. Scranton, Harold Brown, Carla Hills** and **Cyrus Vance,** former Secretary of State. IBM operates in Colombia through a 90%-owned subsidiary, IBM de Columbia S.A.

And note this:

> "*Few of the prisoners working for private companies have been convicted. Rather, they are caught up in the Colombian system of justice, in which the accused usually stays in prison until tried or until he serves time equal to the term he would have received if tried and convicted. Since bail is practically nonexistent, about 75% of the inmates fall into this category. Some have been jailed 8 to 10 years without a trial.*"[24]

The slave labor program is well described by the previously cited Fernando Umana:

> "*This isn't a rehabilitation program at all, just window dressing for what almost amounts to slave labor.*"[25]

Only time and space limit expansion on this theme of Trilateral anti-human rights activities.

TRILATERALS VS. A FREE AMERICA

Trilateralism is the creation of a group of international bankers and multinational corporations. One should not hesitate to criticize these bankers and multinationals for what they are — perverters of individual freedom, and subverters of the Constitution of the United States. But one must not mistake limited criticism of *some* bankers and *some* multinationals for an attack on *all* bankers and multinationals. It is painfully clear that *most* bankers and *most* corporations are not in the slightest involved in the end-run takeover of political power in the United States. The distinction the authors have made is between *most* bankers and businessmen (who operate more or less in a free enterprise system, and respect and want this system) and a small self-perpetuating group that has perverted the system to its own narrow and feudalistic aims.

Take a well-accepted speech by Dr. J. Kirchhoff, president of Castle & Cook Inc., that was reprinted in *Barrons*. In this speech, Kirchhoff lists the "enemies" of capitalism but omits the most important of these enemies — his capitalist peers who have subsidized and nurtured the enemies of the free enterprise system. Says Kirchhoff:

> *"Until the mid 1950's we had a good image. Capitalism could rest on its own merits. We were effective and efficient. No one quarreled with that thesis. Visible proof of its success was witnessed in a high standard of living, political freedom and unlimited economic opportunity. We had no specific five-year plan of action. We did not program the lives of others. We were free to build and to create wherever a free market existed. We were accepted or rejected based on the quality of our performance and workmanship.*
>
> *Such is not the case today: We are required to defend our very existence to a carping melodramatic 'elite minority' that produces absolutely nothing for its fellow man. Few, if any, of this elite ever developed blisters on their hands from any honest, productive labor. I personally refuse to accept the principles of this minority and I refuse to accept as part of corporate life increased government control, corporate abuse, terrorist attacks or other pressure which are being generated by this pseudo elite."*

Apparently some church-related groups, which also happened to be supported by totalitarian capitalists, were attacking Castle and Cooke. Kirchhoff said,

> *"When a church related* [sic] *group contributes $85,000 to terrorist revolutionaries in Rhodesia, who oppose the concept of free elections in a multi-racial society, it forfeits any immunity from criticism."*[26]

We agree. But wait! Who are the prime supporters of these church groups who support terrorism? None other than *some* of Kirchhoff's fellow capitalists. In fact, the speech touches on this:

> *"The guises frequently used are 'The New International Economic Order,' 'Alternative Economic and Social Solutions' and 'Economic Democracy.' These buzz words are palatable, at least on the surface. They are, nonetheless, the siren songs of the Marxist idealogues who have simple, uncomplicated goals: the destruction of the world's most efficient economic machine and the assumption of political power through default."*[27]

Trilateral Paper No. 14 is entitled *Towards a Renovated International System* and outlines a "global strategy" for the "New International Economic Order" castigated by Kirkhhoff.

Other criticism is directed at the World Council of Churches. For example, J. Irwin Miller is chairman of the board of Cummins Engine (Cummins has been a prominent subsidizer of the Soviet Union) as well as a member of the central and executive committees of the World Council of Churches. The WCC regularly votes funds for Marxist-terror groups around the world. In addition, the president of Cummins Engine is Trilateral **Henry Schacht and William Scrantan is a director.**

The World Council of Churches also has a long record of financial support from the Communist world. For example, between 1970 and 1976 East Germany contributed almost $1 million to the WCC. Holland has contributed even more than this to "The fund to combat racism." In practice, of course, the fund has nothing to do with combating racism. Black Africans were threatened with death by WCC-subsidized Marxist groups such as SWAPO, ZANU and the Pan-African Congress: all nine black ministers in the former Rhodesian government received death threats from WCC-supported ZANU, a black Marxist-terrorist group.

This is well documented. Individual members of Western churches affiliated with the WCC must take personal responsibility for this financial support of murder.

Targeting the WCC Kirchhoff comments:

"We must overcome Western civilization's growing sense of guilt. There is nothing evil about profit in spite of the semantic games played by the agitators. If it were not for profit and incentive, the Western world would not be providing food, hard and soft goods, technology, services, and loans to the rest of the world . . .

"The survival of truth and common decency are never certain, and must be fought for constantly. We are at war, but it is a guerilla war. It is being fought in the courtroom, the board room and the media. The enemy is organized, discernible and has ample resources.

"Castle & Cooke does not intend, after 127 years, to forfeit its principles to guerrillas of any political stripe.

"I am convinced that our path, rather than theirs, is the one that offers more hope for the future, but it cannot be accomplished in a vacuum or by one corporation. Let's revitalize our corporate leadership and take the offensive, in the best tradition of American capitalism."[28]

If American capitalists want *public* support they must first clean house. While Mr. Kirchhoff makes good sense, he needs to name names, point out responsibility and challenge J. Irwin Miller and his fellow revolutionaries before calling on aid from the American society at large.

FOOTNOTES CHAPTER 6

1. Vermont Royster, *Orient Express*, Wall Street Journal, February 12, 1980 p. 1.

2. Zbigniew Brzezinski, Washington Star, December 31, 1978, E4.

3. J. Paul Asutin retired as president and operating officer of Coca-Cola on March 1, 1981.

4. The Washington Post, December 24, 1978, p. D4.

5. Richard Cooper, et al., *Toward a Renovated International System*, p. 30.

6. New York Times, June 12, 1921, p. 2 column 3.

7. Reported by AP (Taipei, Taiwan) December 24, 1980.

8. Antony C. Sutton, *Western Technology and Soviet Economic Development, 1917 to 1930*, p. 284.

9. Chihiro Hosoya et al, *Collaboration with Communist Countries in Managing Global Problems: and Examination of the Options.*

10. Robert K. Dornan, *Banking Interests in Panama*, Congressional Record (September 15, 1977).

11. Ibid.

12. *Uneven Justice?*, Wall Street Journal, May 11, 1978, p. 1.

13. George Cornell, AP Report, Arizona Republic, March 10, 1979.

15. Ibid.

16. Reed Irvine, *Behind the News*, Accuracy In Media (1978).

17. Jack Anderson, El Paso Times, April 27, 1978.

18. Ibid.

19. Ibid.

20. Francois Sauzey, *Henry Kissinger*, Trilogue No. 19 (Fall 1978), p. 3.

21. Wall Street Journal, June 20, 1975, p.1.

22. Ibid. p. 1.

23. Ibid. p. 10.

24. Ibid. p. 10.

25. Ibid., p. 25.

26. Dr. J. Kirchhoff, *Corporate Missionary: those who believe in Capitalism must fight back*, Barrons (February 19, 1979), p. 3.

27. Ibid., p. 3.

28. Op. cit., p. 3.

CHAPTER SEVEN

THE PACIFIC BASIN PHENOMENON

Analysts are predicting that the 1980 Reagan presidential election will be a boon for Western states, particularly California. These claims are not unreasonable, for Reagan will naturally sympathize with Western issues much more than **Carter** did. Conversely, **Carter** clearly favored some Southern states during his administration.

But things were already shifting westward, well before Reagan and **Bush** (from the Southwest) were elected. For instance **Alden Clausen,** the chairman of San Francisco-based Bank of America, was appointed by **Carter** (with Reagan's tacit approval) to head the World Bank. Another example is Arizona Governor **Bruce Babbitt's** invitations to join the Trilateral Commission and the Council on Foreign Relations in mid 1980.

While traditionally Westerners have stayed aloof from the Eastern Establishment, it seems that the Eastern Establishment is moving in on the West. Western Trilaterals, notably **David Packard, George Weyerhaeuser, Caspar Weinberger** and others, have grown rapidly in national and international prominence and influence as a result of this transition.

There is a reason for this shift in power, and as always, it is related to economic trade and profits.

In 1979 the dollar amount of US trade with Pacific Basin countries outstripped trade done with Atlantic nations. (This refers to the countries that border the Pacific and Atlantic Oceans, respectively.) One major reason for this is the rapidly expanding Japanese economy; for instance, Japan recently surpassed the US in auto production. The boom in the electronics industry in Taiwan, Korea and other oriental countries is also expanding every month.

To multinational elitists, the hope of the future lies in Mainland (Communist) China, with its 800 million population and virtual slave labor market. There is interest in selling goods and services to the Chinese population, of course, but the potential for making goods in China for export to the rest of the world is overwhelming. Low cost department stores in the US are already carrying Chinese made textile goods that are priced thirty per cent or more *below* any other brands.

China will be a profit bonanza for the multinationals, but a depression for American labor forces who cannot possibly compete with the Chinese wage market. Indeed, China proves to become the great "equalizer" between the "haves" and "have nots" in the world.

International interest is high also. In February 1980 *Business Week* reported:

> "*Japanese Prime Minister Masayoshi Ohira is being urged by some of his liberal, English-speaking advisors to take the initiative in setting up a Pacific Community, modeled on the European Economic Community . . . The Japanese, enthusiastic about the Pacific Community idea, have set up a meeting in Canberra, Australia, this fall to discuss the project.*"[1]

In May 1980, one of the first steps in that direction took place with the response of the Pacific Basin Economic Council (which met in Australia) to a proposed think tank. On May 15, 1980, the *Arizona Republic* reported the following story which was not seen elsewhere. It quoted a prospectus of that planned think tank, the Pacific Basin Institute:

" 'The Pacific Basin Institute will be a private, non-profit research center serving as a focal point for the business communities of North America, South America and Asia, with special emphasis on applied studies concerning trade, investment and economic development in the Pacific Region.

" 'PBI is strategically located in Arizona, which borders Mexico and is the center of the most dynamic growth area in the United States.

" 'The Southwestern site offers easy accessibility for Pacific Basin leaders of business, government and education to come together in an ideal climate with excellent resorts and meeting facilities.'

"The proposed research center is the brainchild of Mallery, who refused to comment on the results of the trip to Australia. . .

"Gov. Bruce Babbitt, who said Phoenix business and government leaders have been working intensively on the idea for a year, said the prospects of the research center becoming a reality look favorable.

" 'Arizona must get into the arena of international trade on a large scale,' he **[Babbitt]** said. 'It must have the academic and research capacity to underpin that kind of effort. That's what this is all about.

" 'The underlying philosophy behind the concept is to look at the Pacific Basin region for data gathering and economic decision-making in partnership with business and government,' he said.

The prospectus says a site for the center 'has been donated and sufficient financing has been committed to construct and operate the facility.'

". . . The prospectus says the business activity and financial affairs of the institute would be directed by a board of trustees made up of 45 persons 'who hold business, government and academic positions is throughout the Pacific region.' "

This sounds similar to many other elite organizations that

desire to make decisions for the rest of the world, but would be of little consequence if the people involved were of little consequence.

The others involved with PBI were revealed in the same article:

> *"The Pacific Basin Economic Council, a federation of private-sector businessmen representing 20 countries, including Canada, Japan, China and New Zealand, met in Sydney, Australia, last week and responded 'very positively' to the concept, said Larry Landry, director of the state* [Arizona] *Office of Economic Planning and Development.*
>
> *"Landry, along with Phoenix lawyer Richard Mallery and Roger Lyon, president of Valley National Bank, went to Australia last week to gain acceptance of the proposed Pacific Basin Institute..²*

The four principals here are Larry Landry, Richard Mallery, Roger Lyon and **Bruce Babbitt.**

Arizona Governor **Bruce Babbitt's** appointment to the Trilateral Commission coincided with the announcement of PBI. **Babbitt** is an old-line Arizona Democrat with direct ties to Washington. He received his degree from Harvard Law School, but only after receiving an advanced degree in geology. He was the only public official appointed by **Carter** to the Kemeny Commission (which investigated the Three Mile Island Incident) and later **Carter** named him to chair the Nuclear Safety Oversight Committee on May 7, 1979.

As head of the Arizona Office of Economic Planning and Development Department, Larry Landry serves directly under **Babbitt.**

Richard Mallery is part of **Babbitt's** tight-knit "Kitchen Cabinet", all of whom were classmates at Harvard. Mallery is described by the March 2, 1980 *Arizona Republic* as "A partner in the prestigious Snell and Wilmer law firm ... shuns active involvement in the Democratic Party. He is viewed as nonpartisan, moves well in both party circles and is more concerned about issues than party dogma."³

Roger A. Lyon however, reveals the most interesting background. Lyon is president of Valley National Bank of Arizona, the 28th largest bank in the country and the largest in the Rocky Mountain Region. The largest individual shareholder in VNB is investment banker J.P. Morgan & Co. of New York, with a whopping 4.2% of VNB's outstanding shares.

In late 1980, Lyon was elected to serve as chairman of the powerful Western Regional Council, which represents "40 of the largest corporations, banks, utilities and other businesses in the Western States," according to the *Arizona Republic*. Lyon had this to say about Western regional interests:

> *"We are different from the east . . . in water, clean air, our vistas, national parks, wildernesses, recreation — we have different values and standards. We have to convince Washington and the rest of the country of that."[4]*

Few asked how Lyon happened to come to Arizona. From 1950 to 1976 (26 years), Lyon served at **David Rockefeller's** Chase Manhattan Bank in New York! Lyon is the third generation of a banking family from New Jersey.

It would appear that Lyon has renounced the East for the sake of Western living, but one might remember the old proverb about a leopard changing its spots.

After analyzing the people who promoted Pacific Basin Institute through the Australian conference, we can see a heavy-weight connection to the Trilateral elite and a typical modus operandi. PBI will have a membership similar to the Trilateral Commission: academics, politicians and multinational corporation "heads of state." Its goal appears similar as well: to foster economic cooperation and trade.

Certainly Pacific Basin Institute is neither a copy nor replacement of the Trilateral Commission. Far from it. More likely it is the result of the same Trilateral policy that opened China up in the first place. Remember, *all* five of the original China negotiators (who worked in secret and included **Carter**), were current or former members of the Trilateral Commission. China is exclusively a Trilateral phenomenon.

Pacific Basin Institute is seen to be the natural extension of that phenomenon. It is certainly something to watch in the future.

It should also be noted at this point that it was very difficult in obtaining information regarding PBI. Governor **Babbitt's** office was totally uncooperative and gave us no information. In fact, after his T.C. appointment was made public in 1980 by the Commission itself, **Babbitt** received so much harsh criticism from Arizonans that his staff responded to callers with "I have no personal knowledge of that." This is a standard dodge when a politician doesn't want to answer the question; they now acknowledge his membership.

Valley National Bank and Roger Lyon's office have also been wholly uncooperative in releasing information on PBI. When asked for a "history sheet" on Lyon (a customary handout for top corporate executives, his aide became defensive and refused to release *any* information.

A contact was made with the Japanese embassy in Washington, D.C., who acknowledged that they had information on PBI. While they had originally agreed to send us information, after two months and two more phone calls, nothing was received.

Finally, after contact with Richard Mallery's office, the prospectus for PBI was obtained. According to that report, Mallery is president of PBI and Lyon is chairman of the board.

There is a substantial link to Stanford University: Weldon B. Gibson is vice-chairman of the board and is executive vice president of SRI International (Stanford Reserch Institute). Trilateral **Arjay Miller** is a director of SRI International. Philip Habib, a senior fellow at Hoover Institution at Stanford is vice president of PBI.

Acknowledgements and thanks were given to heavyweights like **Winston Lord,** president of the Council on Foreign Relations, and Robert Macy, Jr., managing director of Lehman Brothers, Kuhn Loeb.

CONCLUSIONS:

- The West is rapidly growing in Trialteral influence. The election of Reagan and **Bush** will accelerate this trend.

- As China's manufacturing capacity is brought on line by Trilateral multinational corporations, America (and the rest of the world) will be flooded with noncompetitively priced goods.
- American labor will feel the biggest brunt of this and will lose countless jobs at the expense of Chinese slave labor.
- The Pacific Basin Institute is the main instrument that will be used by the Trilateral elite to coordinate the Pacific Basin and to devise and recommend "policies" for participating countries in the Basin.

FOOTNOTES CHAPTER 7

1. Maryanne McNellis, *Japan's Push for a Pacific Community,* Business Week (February 25, 1980), p. 72.

2. Joel Nilsson, *Pacific Region Businessmen Back Idea of State-Based Trade Institute,* Arizona Republic (May 15, 1980), p. A-1.

3. *Richard Mallery: Bridge to the business community,* Arizona Republic (March 2, 1980), P. A-1.

4. J.J. Casserly, *Bank Chief to Lead Regional Council,* Arizona Republic (December 6, 1980).

CHAPTER EIGHT

BACKWARD
AND FORWARD

At this point we should step back and look at the Trilateral Commission in the light of history. The Commission represents the third attempt by the New York international banking fraternity to create a New Economic World Order under their control. When we look at this third attempt within the context of history, it is clear why the Commission (or its equivalent) will continue.

THE ORIGINS OF GLOBALISM

It was Thomas Jefferson, writer and signer of the Declaration of Independence who first warned a newly independent America about the powers behind the scenes of government:

"If the American people ever allowed the banks to control the issuance of their currency, first by inflation and then by deflation, the banks and corporations that will grow up around them will deprive the people of all property until their children will wake up homeless on the continent their fathers occupied. The issuing power

of money should be taken from the banks and restored to Congress and the people to whom it belongs.

"I sincerely believe the banking institutions are more dangerous to liberty than standing armies."[1]

The "banking institutions" are represented today by Trilateralism. What was true in 1790 is true in 1980.

Out of seventy-seven Trilateral commissioners, well over one-half are either directors of banks, or have been directors of the Federal Reserve System (which is owned and controlled by private banks). We also must recall that **David Rockefeller,** chairman of Chase Manhattan Bank, founded the Trilateral Commission.

To follow through on Thomas Jefferson's prophetic warning, "the American people" have not merely allowed "banks to control the issuance of their currency," but almost unbelievably they have allowed banking interests to control the domestic and foreign policies of the United States.

ATTEMPT #1: THE LEAGUE OF NATIONS

The formal attempt to extend control of the United States to the world was the League of Nations. The idea for the League of Nations came from Cecil Rhodes' Round Table groups and was proposed to Woodrow Wilson at least as early as September 1915 by Sir Edward Grey, a member of the Round Table, in a letter to Colonel M. House:

"Would the President propose that there should be a League of Nations binding themselves to side against any power which broke a treaty."[2]

What went wrong with the League of Nations? Elitists blame the failure on Woodrow Wilson. For example, elitist academic Harlan Cleveland wrote:

"The first try, the League of Nations, was the product of Woodrow Wilson's strong initiative and the victim of his weak follow through: the United States wrote most of the club rules, then decided not to join the club. In its weakened condition, it could not survive the rise of fascism, Naziism and militarism."[3]

This statement is typical of elitist evasion and distortion of truth. Cleveland makes at least the following errors:

- The League did not survive Hitler to be sure, but who financed and nurtured Hitler? None other than key members of the Council on Foreign Relations, the successor to the Inquiry which promoted the League. (See Antony Sutton, *Wall Street and The Rise of Hitler.*)

- Cleveland does not mention that the rise of Communism was also financed and nurtured by the same key members of the Council on Foreign Relations. (See Antony Sutton, *Wall Street and the Bolshevik Revolution.*)

- It is more valid to argue that the first try at New Economic World Order failed because the "club" saw more profit (both financially and for the goal of New Economic World Order) in the Second World War. This aspect of world history has to be buried because it would highlight the amoral character of elitists.

ATTEMPT #2: THE COUNCIL ON FOREIGN RELATIONS

In New York, July 29, 1921, the elite founded a semi-secret organization called The Council on Foreign Relations. The CFR evolved out of the American Delegation to the Paris Peace Conference in 1919, which later merged with the American Branch of the British Institute of International Affairs. This culminated with the formation of the United Nations. The report of the founding committee for the CFR contained the following statement of purpose:

> *"Until recent years it was usual to assume that in foreign affairs each government must think mainly, if not entirely, of the interests of its own people. In founding the League of Nations the allied powers have now recognized that national policies ought to be framed with an eye to the welfare of society at large."*[4]

Here we have precisely the same globalist objective to be

found in the Trilateral Commission today.

What is important is the makeup of the board of directors of the Council on Foreign Relations during the 1920's and 1930's. It was dominated, as is the Trilateral Commission, by Wall Street banking interests.

Prominent among the early directors was Paul M. Warburg, partner in the firm of Kuhn-Loeb and the first member appointed by Woodrow Wilson to the Federal Reserve Board. In fact, Warburg was the brains behind the Federal Reserve System. Warburg was also chairman of the International Acceptance Bank, Inc. and (much less known) a director of American I.G. Chemical Corporation which was the American branch of I.G. Farben that had so much to do with the rise of Hitler.

In the Trilateral Commission today we find Kuhn-Loeb and the Federal Reserve System well represented. **Charles W. Robinson,** former managing director of Kuhn-Loeb, was in the **Carter** administration. Links between Trilateralism and Federal Reserve System include **Arthur F. Burns, Andrew Brimmer, David Rockefeller, Paul Volcker, Bruce K. MacLaury, Alden Clausen** and **Robert V. Roosa.**

Another Wall Street financier on the board of the CFR was Otto H. Kahn. Like Paul Warburg, Kahn was a former partner in the private banking company of Kuhn-Loeb. Russell C. Leffingwell was a director of the Council on Foreign Relations during the inter-war years.. In 1919 he held the office of Secretary of the Treasury and had been in partnership with J.P. Morgan and Company.

Another director of the CFR was Owen D. Young, chairman of General Electric Company (which was dominated by the J.P. Morgan interests) and the German Reparations Committee (which drew up the so-called Young Plan). CFR director Allan W. Dulles served during the inter-war period. During the same time, Dulles was also a director of J. Henry Schroeder Banking Corporation and a partner in the establishment law firm of Solomon and Cromwell. It is recorded that the J. Henry Schroeder Banking firm was one of the key elements behind the rise of Hitler in Germany.

Another inter-war director of the CFR was Norman H.

Davis. According to Q
the Morgans."[5] He had
Paris Peace Delegation. W
1913 financial backing for the
life long friend." Cleveland Hoa
National City Bank and the Russe

The CFR exerted its major influenc
1940 through the mid 1960's, and its mem
all of the establishment leaders particularl
Street banker John J. McCloy, John Foste
Dulles and so on. The high point of the CFR und
the creation of the United Nations. John D. Rock
donated the New York site and was instrumental in ge
United Nations off the ground in San Francisco in 194

At the height of CFR powers in 1971, a dispute over the edit
of the Council's quarterly *Foreign Affairs* magazine marked the
end of the second attempt for new world order. Under President
Bayless Manning, a former dean of the Stanford Law School,
the CFR tried to broaden its membership from a geographical,
age, racial and sexual standpoint. By the 1970's the CFR had
sixty women and twenty-two blacks on its rolls; but these new
members were not selected as carefully as in the past and the
expertise and prestige traditionally associated with the CFR
was diluted. When Manning attempted to appoint William P.
Bundy to the editorship of *Foreign Affairs*, he (Manning) was
eased out of the CFR presidency by **David Rockefeller.**

ATTEMPT #3: TRILATERALISM

In 1973 the third attempt at new world order came under the
guise of the Trilateral Commission. It had different short- and
medium-term objectives than both the League of Nations and
United Nations.

Trilateralism abandons the concept of bringing together
nations into a *political* world society in one giant step. Instead,
it proposes to first create regional economic groupings and then
link the three most important of these regional groupings
(North America, Europe and Japan) into a *new economic world
order*. The discussion and policy-making steps necessary for

:orpora-
ired but

FR allies

ems, not
merican

nge the
ir ends.
Ages, p.

iver-
e tar-
n *the*

Order is
impossible as long as the Constitution exists in its present form. More dictatorial powers are needed to function as revealed in an official Commission report:

> *"If a more effective and equitable economic order is to emerge, national policies and programs must be subject to moderation and adjustment to take into account probable adverse international ramifications. This can be accomplished only if powerful domestic agencies are brought under control and sensitized to the international consequences of their policies."*[7]

The Trilateral Commission here proposes that our domestic policies be subordinated to international policies.

In *The Crisis of Democracy* (funded and written by the Trilateral Commission) evidence is found that Trilaterals need to restrict Constitutional freedoms. For example, the right to free speech is protected under the First Amendment to the Constitution. Yet the following concerning freedom of the press is found:

> *". . . it is a freedom which can be abused. . . . the responsibility of the press should now be increased to be commensurate with its power, significant measures are*

[Rotated marginal text:]

...uigley, Davis was a "non-legal agent of
...represented the US Treasury on the
...oodrow Wilson himself owed his
...Presidency to his "classmate and
...ley Dodge was a director of
...Sage Foundation.
...during the period from
...bers reflected almost
...people like Wall
...Dulles, Allen
...oubtedly was
...efeller, Sr.
...ing the

required to restore an appropriate balance between the press, the governments and other institutions in society."8

How does the Commission propose to do this?

". . . beginning with the Interstate Commerce Commission and the Sherman Anti-Trust Act measures had to be taken to regulate the new industrial centers of power and define their relations to the rest of society. Something comparable appears to be now needed with respect to the media."9

Of course, monopoly of industry and commerce is not the same as freedom of speech. The break-up of monopoly cannot in any way be compared to restrictions on expressions of ideas. It is a logical absurdity, yet an excellent example of Trilateral use of non sequiturs.

THE 1980's PROJECT

Continuation of the Trilateral Commission is almost a foregone conclusion. The Trilateral process is simply another attempt in almost 100 years of new world order plans.

There are subtle but important changes in Trilateralism to be noted. Not only is the immediate objective limited to regional groupings but the Trilateral program is carefully balanced on two key hinges:

a. That a New Economic World Order is inevitable. For example, "The management of interdependence has become indispensable for world order in the coming years. Its origins lie in the extraordinary expansion of interaction between modern states and societies."10

b. That the objective can be attained through propaganda techniques. To this end, almost endless studies and reports are published assuming that the New Economic World order is inevitable for the survivial of mankind. This assumption is critical because it has no basis in fact.

It is notable that the major propaganda effort is still centered within the Council on Foreign Relations i.e., the 1980's Project. But the clue to Trialteral involvement is their dominance of the

CFR Committee on Studies responsible for the 1980's Project.

So far, the project consists of twenty-five volumes released by McGraw-Hill. They lay down the "steering trends" to new world order in the 1980's. Of the ten members of the CFR Committee on Studies, four were Trilaterals (**Kissinger, Volcker, Whitman, Perkins**). The chairman was **Perkins** — **Kissinger** and **Volcker** dominated the other members (pedestrian academics without fame or notoriety).

TRILATERAL MONEY MANAGEMENT

No doubt by this time readers will have grasped the fundamental observation that the Trilateral New Economic World Order is intended for the private benefit of Trialteral Commissioners at the expense of everyone else. This is the secret of monopoly, possibly age old, but certainly rediscovered by the Rockefeller-Morgan financial elite at the end of the 19th century.

Trilaterals are just following the golden rule of John D. Rockefeller, Sr. and John Pierpoint Morgan: gain political power and use it for financial objectives.

If this is the fundamental Trilateral rule, what can be said about the future of our society? Specifically on monetary affairs, the following can be projected:

- A fiat currency. This is absolutely essential for the New Economic World Order, and must be coupled with international fiat "reserve" assets.

- Gold will continue to be centralized into a few hands. Gold in the hands of the many is out of the question if Trilateralism is to succeed. As gold provides for personal economic sovereignty, it must be retained in the hands of the elitist few and directly or indirectly be controlled.

The Treasury campaign to demonetize gold, formerly led by Trilateral **W. Michael Blumenthal,** is an admission that Trilaterals are having problems in this segment of their program.

Gold has been removed from our monetary system in order to

remove the shackles from "management" (manipulation) of the monetary system for elitist objectives. This policy was begun by Franklin D. Roosevelt in 1933 and it must not be forgotten that Roosevelt himself, far from being a man of the people, came from the old established banking family that created the Bank of New York in 1784.

The Repeal of the *1933 Joint Resolution* by Congress in 1974 has allowed American citizens to privately own gold, but was coupled with a Treasury program to sell gold and depress its price. Under US dominance, the International Monetary Fund joined in the gold-selling campaign. These selling pressures temporarily held down the price of gold.

Crisis management (or problem management) is an essential Trialteral tool to build a New Economic World Order. Problems do not exist to be solved or ameliorated. Problems exist to exasperate, knowingly or unknowingly in order to advance basic world order objectives.

Monetary management is no exception. Trilateralist proposals for monetary management will not solve the questions of inflation, federal intervention, burdensome taxation, interest rates or any other matter.

One may be justified in thinking that academic experts in the Trilateral Commission are chosen because their "solutions" coincide with the objectives of the power elite. An excellent example is found in the views of **Gardner Ackley** who is a member of the Commission as well as having held the position of professor of political economy at Henry Carter University and the University of Michigan. An interview with **Ackley** presents **Ackley** as a valuable asset for Trilateralism. His proposals advance New Economic World Order objectives:

> *"There are many occasions in which deficits are appropriate and necessary . . . There are many occasions in which deficits are unavoidable."*[11]

THE 1980 PRESIDENTIAL ELECTIONS

Trilateralism was heavily represented in every major political campaign in 1980. **John Anderson** — running on an independent ticket — was a member of the Commission and was duly financed by many individual fellow members. **Jimmy Carter** and **Walter Mondale** both had definite connections with the Commission.

While Ronald Reagan was not a member of the Trilateral Commission, many of his top campaign advisors were. We want to demonstrate how Trilateralism "covered all the bets" in the political arena, and how its resulting influence on Ronald Reagan — the victor— will all but guarantee the success of their New Economic World Order plans.

By the time the Republican National Convention met to nominate a candidate, Ronald Reagan had no serious rival. Excitement was high because for the first time in a long time there was a unified party. Senator Barry Goldwater delivered a well-cheered speech stating the dangers of elitist influence in government — he also said that this might be the last election America faces.

Goldwater's recent book, *With No Apologies*, devotes an entire chapter to the Trilateral Commission. Without judging his intent, we can safely say that Goldwater well understands the Trilateral Commission and its goals.

Goldwater's speech was cheered but his warnings were ignored. After the convention forcefully rejected **Kissinger's** proposal for a "split Presidency" (with **Kissinger** being the "other" president), it turned right around and nominated Trilateral **George Bush** for Reagan's vice-presidential running mate.

After this, many prominent and hopeful conservatives "counselled" the authors that Reagan was not connected to the Trilaterals and would "use" anything or anybody he could to get elected. In the Trilaterals' case, it was OK because Reagan would quickly dispense with them once he was elected.

One of the largest pro-Reagan forces in the country was Moral Majority, a quasi-Christian political action group originally brainstormed by Paul Weyrich in Washington. Other groups like Moral Majority (Round Table and Christian Voice, for example) were wooed by Reagan in typical political fashion.

After the election, millions of Americans (many of whom

are fundamental Christians) were looking to Reagan to support their positions. But the November 24 issue of *U.S. News & World Report* revealed the hard reality:

> "*Top officials of the Reagan team have sent a message to the Moral Majority: 'It isn't your administration.' These advisers to the President-elect are urging him to ignore political threats of punishment by the religious right if he does not support their policies.*"[12]

The article went on to say:

> "*Reagan's first moves after the November 4 election generally pleased moderate Republicans and Democrats, some of whom feared he would follow the dictates of his most conservative supporters. 'Hell with them,' Vice President-elect George Bush declared on November 10 in Houston, referring to right-wing groups that supported the President-elect.*"[13]

In perspective then one must ask, "Who is going to throw whom out of where?"

America had bought the "anti-elitist" story once more, like they did with CFR member Franklin Delano Roosevelt in 1934 and Trilateral **Jimmy Carter** in 1976. The facts cannot be ignored: Reagan's campaign was engineered and operated by Trilaterals **David Packard, George Weyerhaeuser, Bill Brock, Anne Armstrong** and **Caspar Weinberger,** and a large assortment of CFR members. Reagan was personally supported by **David Rockefeller.**

WILL THE REAL REAGAN PLEASE STAND UP?

On November 6, 1980, the following Reagan quote was widely reported in the nation's press:

> "*I think there is an elite in this country and they are the very ones who run an elitist government. They want a government by a handful of people because they don't believe the people themselves can run their lives. . . . Are we going to have an elitist government that makes decisions for peoples' lives, or are we going to believe as we have for so many decades, that the people can make these decisions for themselves?*"[14]

Reagan certainly cannot claim ignorance of the scope and influence of the Trilateral Commission. Indeed, he has been rubbing elbows with the Eastern elite for many years as a member of the exclusive male-only Bohemian Grove Club in Northern California.

The San Mateo Times quoted Irving Stone, the author of *The Origin* — a biographical novel of evolutionist Charles Darwin — and an ardent evolutionist. In light of Reagan's wooing non-evolutionists (i.e., the before-mentioned fundamental groups) during the campaign, Stone's comments serves as another warning that things might not be as they appear.

> *"I've known Ronald Reagan for 35 years. He's a very warm, personable man. But Ronnie doesn't have the mind to make independent judgements . . . he has to have a script which he will memorize perfectly.*
>
> *"I'm a little frightened to have a man in the Oval Office who can't make independent judgements. . . When he made that statement about evolution in Houston, he was talking to a large crowd of Fundamentalists. Apparently, he wants their votes very badly."[15]*

After the election, Reagan assembled a "transition team" which would later select, screen and recommend appointees for major administration posts. According to a compilation by *Research Publications* of Phoenix, of the fifty-nine people Reagan named to that team, twenty-eight were members of the CFR, ten belonged to the secret and elite Bilderberger group, and no less than ten were Trilaterals.

There are two particular "brain trusts" that will fuel Reagan's foreign policy. The first is Stanford University's Hoover Institution on War, Revolution and Peace in Palo Alto, California. The other is Georgetown University's Center for Strategic and International Studies (CSIS) in Washington, D.C. Almost forty of the total transition team had been associated with one or the other of these "think tanks." Reportedly, fifteen of Reagan's advisors came from CSIS. (**Henry Kissinger** is a professor at CSIS, for instance.)

The chairman of CSIS is Trilateral **David M. Abshire**, who also headed Reagan's foreign policy and defense transition staff.

David Packard is the most influential overseer at the Hoover Institution at Stanford.

In short, the reader can see that regardless of good intentions or wishful thinking, Reagan appears to be totally consumed by Trilaterals. This is the Trilateral way of political "protection." A Reagan-**Bush** administration will result in further progress for Trilaterals toward their New Economic World Order:

- Reagan will stress business and economics, and "business" is the Trilaterals' expertise.

- The new Republican majority Senate will be very cooperative with the administration as far as an economic policy is concerned.

- Under Democratic control, Trilateral headway was stagnating; it has a "fresh start" with Republican control. Here we apply the principle that a ship will not respond to rudder control unless substantial movement is present.

Looking to the next ten years in light of the last sixty years does not promise anything but "business as usual." The same type of elite groups that dominated in the 1920's are dominating today. They are moving forward today with no less resolve than they were then. And prospects for their success never looked brighter.

FOOTNOTES CHAPTER 8

1. Thomas Jefferson, *The Writings of Thomas Jefferson*, (Autobiography, correspondence, reports messages addresses and other writings.) vol. 7, p. 685.

2. Jennings C. Wise, *Woodrow Wilson: Disciple of Revolution*, p. 382.

3. Harlan Cleveland, *The Third Try at World Order*, p. 2.

4. Whitney H. Shepardson, *Early History of the Council on Foreign Relations*, p. 3.

5. Carroll Quigley, *Tragedy and Hope*, p. 50.

6. Zbigniew Brzezinski, *Between Two Ages: America's Role in the Technetronic Era*, p. 258.

7. Egidio Ortona and et.al., *The Problem of International Consulations*, p. 17.

8. Michael Crozier and et.al., *The Crisis of Democracy*, p. 181.

9. Ibid., p. 182.

10. Richard Cooper and et.al., *Toward a Renovated International System*, p. 4.

11. *A Constitutional Ban On Red Ink?*, U.S. News & World Report, January 29, 1979, p. 27.

12. *Washington Whispers,* U.S. News & World Report vol. LXXXIX No. 21 (November 24, 1980), p. 20.

13. Ibid., p. 22.

14. San Jose Mercury, November 6, 1980.

15. San Mateo Times, October 16, 1980.

CHAPTER NINE

TRILATERALISM IN EUROPE

Trilateralism, as its name suggests, is a three-sided affair:
(a) The United States
(b) Japan
(c) Western Europe (excluding Austria, Greece, and Sweden)

This area includes eighty percent of the economic power in the non-Communist world and is the source of virtually all of the world's new technology.

The basic Trilateral concept is to link the three economic power areas in the world into a united international force. US dominance would mean **Rockefeller**-Chase Manhattan dominance because Trilateralism was created by **David Rockefeller** and continues to be dominated by him.

The European segment of the Commission shares the same goals for a New Economic World Order, but they would envision themselves as the ultimate dominating factor (likewise for the Japanese Trilaterals).

The political gaps in Trilateral distribution are more than noticeable. Africa is not included. Neither is the Far East, Latin America or Australasia.

Trilaterals want to build a unified Trilateral force, then draw in the last named areas on a piecemeal basis. Africa (apart from South Africa) is undeveloped and contributes talk rather than power. The Far East is a complex emerging economic force. Australasia is not powerful in global terms.

Latin America includes some powerful countries (Brazil, Argentina and Mexico) — yet is ignored because the Latin cultural tradition has kept Latin leaders aware of Chase Manhattan-**Rockefeller** activities. In general, Europe has a residue of gratitude for World War II, while Latin America has a long standing cultural antipathy towards anything smacking of international banking operators: Catholic bankers, for instance, are bound by religious precepts to lend money for productive purpose only. New York bankers use money and debt for political control.

Each Trilateral area has a chairman and a deputy chairman. **David Rockefeller** is North American chairman and **Mitchell Sharp** of Canada is North American deputy chairman. Europeans hold these positions for their Trilateral side:

Georges Berthoin is European chairman

Egidio Ortona is European deputy chairman

Berthoin is president of the European Movement and one time aide to Jean Monnet, father of "One Europe." **Egidio Ortona** is president of Honeywell Information Systems, Italia, which is closely linked to Trilateral **Edson W. Spencer,** president of Honeywell in the US.

The geographical distribution of Trilateralists in Europe is shown in Table 1.

TABLE I
GEOGRAPHICAL DISTRIBUTION OF EUROPEAN TRILATERALS

COUNTRY	NUMBER OF TRILATERAL COMMISSIONERS	EXECUTIVE COMMITTEE MEMBERS	NUMBER IN "PUBLIC SERVICE"
UNITED KINGDOM	26	2	2
W. GERMANY	21	3	2
FRANCE	18	3	4
ITALY	15	3	2
EIRE (IRELAND)	7	1	2
NORWAY	3	1	1
NETHERLANDS	6	1	0
DENMARK	3	1	2
SPAIN	12	2	0
PORTUGAL	3	0	0
TOTAL	114	17	15

TRILATERALISM AND "ONE EUROPE"

The link between "One Europe," or a United States of Europe and Trilateralism is important. To move from three regional groupings to "One World" requires that each region be cohesive and unified. (Authors' note: "One Europe" is an established term created by the people associated with it. "One World" is the authors' coinage to compare and describe the larger concept.) This is impossible with the current state of the United Nations. It is much more plausible in the Trilateral process.

US-Trilateral intent is to build "One Europe" to be merged into a global society. Oddly, this is not the view from Europe, which sees "One Europe" as a final goal. Wall Street sees "One Europe" as a stepping stone to One World.

When links between the European Economic Community (EEC) and Trilaterals are described, the step by step movement towards One World becomes apparent.

There may well be economic arguments for reducing European customs barriers to encourage free trade. But European political disadvantages have been obscured by more superficial economic benefits. To avoid sinking into the Trilateral morass, Europe will have to restrict cooperation to economic and military activities. To extend the cooperative process into the political arena invites loss of European sovereignty to a Trilateral global society. Traditional French hostility towards American political moves is not altogether without foundation.

So with this in mind, the coauthors feel it is important to take a look at European Trilaterals and their links to EEC and "One Europe."

THE EUROPEAN ECONOMIC COMMUNITY

The European Economic Community currently consists of ten countries: Belgium, Denmark, Ireland, France, Germany, Italy, Luxembourg, Netherlands, United Kingdom and Greece. (Greece became an official member as of January 1, 1981.) Spain and Portugal are tentatively slated to join the EEC in 1983.

BELGIUM

Out of ten Belgian Trilaterals, two are prominently connected with Europeanization and two more are connected with international banking.

Henri Simonet is foreign minister of Belgium and immediately before that (1973-1977) was vice president of the European Economic Community (EEC).

Jean Rey was Belgian minister for economic affairs from 1954-1958 followed by a long career at various European Community posts:

- 1958-1967, president of external relations of EEC
- 1967-1970, president of the executive committe of EEC

Two prominent Belgian Trilateral bankers include **Baron Leon Lambert,** president of Groupe Bruxelles Lambert, S A , which is affiliated with the Rothschilds, and **Luc Wauters,** chairman of Groupe Almanij-Kredietbank of Brussels.

DENMARK

There are three Danish Trilaterals. **Svend Auken** is Minister of Labor and was a member of the Committee of Social Democrats *against* EEC to 1971-72. On the other hand, Trilateral **Ivar**

Norgaard is Minister of Environment and was vice president of the European Parliament in 1974. **Norgaard** was a member of the Danish National Bank in 1968 but otherwise Danish Trilaterals are politicians rather than bankers.

EIRE (IRELAND)

There are seven Irish Trilaterals including prominent members of European organizations.

Michael O'Kennedy is the Irish Minister for Foreign Affairs and a former vice president of the Irish Council of the European Party in the senate. Another politician, **M.T.W. Robinson,** is a member of the executive committee of the European Movement. **F. Boland,** chairman of IBM-Ireland and a director of the Investment Bank of Ireland, is a former representative to the United Nations (1956-1964).

The key statement on "Political Cooperation" in the European Community was published by an Irish Trilateral **Garret FitzGerald,** former foreign minister of Ireland and current leader of the Fine Gael opposition party. He asserts that most European political activity is not part of the formal structure of EEC.[1]

Political cooperation is centered in the office of the revolving post of president of the EEC Council of Ministers. A permanent secretariat of some 200 committees is constantly at work and meets on a continuing basis. **FitzGerald** is one-time president of the EEC Council of Ministers and claims that considerable political activity is taking place towards "One Europe." It is notable that according to **FitzGerald, Henry Kissinger** found Europeanization too complex to grasp: *it is a groping, slow movement toward a declaration of European identity.*

FitzGerald concluded:

> ". . . *the work of political cooperation is important because it is only through this pragmatic process of seeking on a piecemeal basis to harmonize foreign policy that that foundation can be laid for a European Community that can eventually develop into a genuine federation or confederation.*"[2]

FRANCE

The French Trilateral component is not truly French but represents mainly the French connection to international and European organizations plus French banking interests.

Trilateralism is totally inconsistent with a deeply held sense of French nationalism. French Trilaterals are much further from the cultural soul of their country than perhaps any other Trilaterals.

The three French Trilateral-European Community links are of major significance. **Raymond Barre,** prime minister and Minister of France, was formerly vice president for Economic and Social Affairs at EEC. **G. Berthoin,** Trilateral European chairman, was the chief EEC representative to the United Kingdom, and was private secretary to the father of the One Europe concept — Jean Monnet. **Robert Marjolin** was formerly vice president of the Commission of the European Communities and was a member of the International Advisory Committee of the Chase Manhattan Bank. **Marjolin** was for many years connected with the EEC and the organization of the OEEC, and with **Berthoin,** he forms the core link between French Trilateralism, the European Economic Community and **David Rockefeller.**

Why does France, the most independent nationalistic nation in Europe — almost the world — produce the strongest single Trilateral link to **David Rockefeller?** The answer might be that the Trilateral Executive Committee recognized the problem of French nationalism as standing in the way of One Europe and One World; perhaps special efforts were made to ensure a powerful French connection.

This French Trilateral triad is backed up by numerous lesser French Trilaterals with One Europe connections. They include **R. Bonety,** formerly with the EEC, **Paul Delouvrier,** formerly with the European Iron and Steel Commission, a part of EEC, and **Francois Duchene,** a French Trilateral residing in England as director of the Center for Contemporary European Studies at the University of Sussex. (This might be termed a European Trilateral think tank on a minor scale.) **Michel Gaudet** was formerly director general of the EEC legal service. **Thierry De Montbrial** is director of the Institut Francais des Relations

Internationales in Paris. This is the French affiliate to the Royal Institute of International Affairs with Trilateral connections through **Sir Andrew Shonfield.** Lastly, there is **Roger Seydoux,** formerly with UNESCO and UN.

Out of twenty-seven French Trilaterals we find that nine have strong One Europe connections.

WEST GERMANY

The West German team of twenty-one Trilaterals includes **Count Otto Lambsdorff,** the German Minister of Economics. In general, West German Trilaterals stress industrial and trade union connections rather than One Europe connections.

Trade unionists include **K. Hauenschild** (Chemical, Paper and Pottery Workers), **E. Loderer** (Metal Workers Union) and **H.O. Vetter** (Federation of Trade Unions).

Industrialists with U.S. connections include **Otto Wolff,** a director of EXXON and a member of the secret Bilderberger group.

Bank directors include **H.K. Jannott, A. Munchmeyer** and **N. Kloten.**

No German Trilaterals have more than incidental connections with One Europe. Even politician Trilaterals in Germany are domestically oriented, for example, **K.H. Narjes, H.J. Junghans and O. Sund.** The only major exception to this observation is **Karl Kaiser,** director of the Research Institute of the German Society for Foreign Policy and who is widely reported abroad and in West Germany.

ITALY

By contrast to West Germany, Italy has a major EEC and One Europe representation.

These Italian Trilaterals include:

- **F. Bobba,** in 1950, was with the Italian Ministry of Foreign Affairs with responsibility for European integration. Later **Bobba** became director general of Economic and Financial Affairs at EEC.
- **Guido Carli** is a longtime member of the EEC Monetary Committee.

- **Umberto Colombo** is a director of the Committee for Scientific Policy at OECD.
- **G. Colonna Di Paliano** has been with a variety of European organizations since 1964, including EEC, ECSC and Euratom. He is also a director of EXXON.
- **E. Ortona** is a former president of the UN Security Council and a president of Honeywell Information Systems (Italia).
- **Giovanni Agnelli** is a key Trilateral, president of Fiat and on the International Advisory committee of Chase Manhattan (**Henry Kissinger** is chairman of the IAC).

LUXEMBOURG
Although an important member of the European Community, Luxembourg has no Trilateral members.

NETHERLANDS
With six Trilaterals, Netherlands has several connected with One Europe including:

M. Kohnstamm, a civil servant with the ECSC in the 1950's and a vice president of the Action Committee of the United States of Europe since 1956.

J. Loudon is a member of the Atlantic Institute and Ford Foundation, a member of the Chase Manhattan International Advisory committee and chairman of Royal Dutch Shell.

E. Wellenstein was with ECSC from 1953-1967 and director General of External Relations at EEC from 1973-1976.

UNITED KINGDOM
With twenty-six Trilateralists, Great Britain has several with a close connection to EEC Affairs. These include:

R.H. Grierson, director general of Industrial and Technical Affairs at EEC in 1973-74.

R. Maudling, with EEC in 1958-59.

C. O'Neill, ambassador to EEC in 1963-66 and a

director of the "Britain in Europe Campaign" 1974-75.

Lord Harlech, chairman of the European Movement.

A.L. Williams, deputy director of European Movement 1970-71.

In brief then, there is (a) except in the case of West Germany, a major connection between One Europe and Trilateralism, and (b) a rather deep connection between Chase Manhattan and the European side of Trilateralism.

HOW EUROPE SEES THE POLITICAL PROCESS

In some ways Europeans have a more sophisticated understanding of the realities of the world political process than many Americans. Yet in other ways Europeans are quite deficient in their understanding of the political workings of both the United States and the Soviet Union.

Historically, Europe has usually been run by elites. Populism in the American tradition does not exist in Europe — it is more of a frontier phenomenon, in the Jefferson-Jackson tradition. Elites are known and hardly mysterious for Europeans. In Britain, for example, the word "establishment" is generally accepted, if not approved, and no one uses the label "paranoid" or "conspiratorialist" to an argument based on acceptance of an Establishment.

For many years in the United States any talk of "elites" or "establishment" put the speaker into the "kook" category. Europe doesn't have to be convinced of the existence of an elite; it is accepted.

From a European perspective, the distinction between Republican and Democrat has always been elusive. The major American parties are seen as merely different sides of the same coin, and the existence of a supra-party elite is quite acceptable.

So it is easier for Europeans to accept the concept of Trilateralism as a verifiable fact. Trilateral human rights policies are seen more clearly in Europe as a pragmatic diplomatic tool. Consequently Germany and France have been major supporters of South Africa, knowing full well that the US elitist attack on South Africa has been motivated by self-interest, not human rights.

Where Europe is weak is in its knowledge of the *details* of American elitism. While the concept is acceptable, knowledge of the details is vague, hazy and perhaps largely unknown.

EUROPEAN BLOCKAGES TO INFORMATION

Rather ironically though, Europe has greater blocks to details of US elitist operations than the United States. Governments own most of the radio and television industry — this means censorship. A program on French radio or television exposing Trilateralism and its meaning for Europe is unthinkable; after all, an important part of the European elite is also Trilateral. French critics such as Pierre de Villamarest have a harder time disseminating information than critics in the United States.

Elitism in Europe is more securely entrenched than in the US. Both the US Constitution and American traditions frown on aristocracies and the flowering American aristocracy that stems from Alexander Hamilton.

ASPEN INSTITUTE BERLIN

The implementation of the concepts of secular humanism in Europe is being achieved through a branch of the Aspen Institute for Humanistic Studies, Trilateralists and other elitists. (See Chapters Two and Three.) This is a major connection between European Trilateralism and American Trilateralism. In 1974, the Aspen Institute Berlin was founded as "an integral part of the Aspen Institute for Humanistic Studies" and serves as the European and non-US funnel through which Trilateral ideas flow. In particular, the Aspen Institute Berlin states its purpose "as a flexible and experimental effort to articulate and to strengthen individual and social *adherance* to humanistic values."[3] (Emphasis added.) In other words, they are trying to force their values on Europe as well.

Members of the board of Aspen Institute Berlin include a host of Trilateralists, humanists, elitists and "One Europe" advocates: **Georges Berthoin** fits all those labels. Another board member is Marion Countess Donhoff, the publisher of *Die Zeit,* whose editor-in-chief is Trilateralist **Theo Sommer,** a participant in **Henry Kissinger's** International Seminar in 1960. **Thierry De Montbrial** was at one time affiliated with the University of California at Berkeley and is the author of books on world economy and energy policy. **Richard Lowenthal,** a professor emeritus at the Free University of Berlin, has taught at elitist schools like University of California at Berkeley, Columbia (where **Brzezinski** had planned to return in January, 1981), Harvard and Stanford, and is an expert on foreign policy, especially in regard to the Communist bloc.

Other non-Trilateral elitists on the board of Aspen-Berlin whom we wish to mention are: Robert McNamara, president, World Bank; Robert O. Anderson, chairman, Aspen Institute and Atlantic Richfield; Pehr Gyllenhammaer, president, Volvo; Conor Cruise O'Brien, editor-in-chief, *The Observer,* London; Jean-Francois Revel, editor, *L'Express,* Paris.

Additionally, we find the two most prominent German politicians of our time on the honorary board. First, there is Willy Brandt, former Federal Chancellor, chairman of the ruling Social Democratic Party and chairman of the United Nations' Independent Commission on International Development Issues (which included **Peter G. Peterson, Henry Kissinger** and *Washington Post* publisher Katherine Graham). Secondly, there is Helmut Schmidt, Chancellor of the Federal Republic of Germany, a close friend of Valery Giscard d'Estaing.

Willy Brandt, in describing the reasoning for the Aspen Institute Berlin's location, gave away his own lack of understanding of the threat of the Communist bloc when he stated, "The choice of Berlin is not accidental — we regard it as a crossroads and touchstone of the new relationship between East and West." More recently, a publication of the Aspen Institute Berlin reported, "Scholars and public figures from the Soviet Union and other countries of Eastern Europe actively participate in the work of the Aspen Institute Berlin."[5] Once again, we view the Trilateralist's naivete and self-serving attitude.

In sum, The Aspen Institute Berlin is a European mirror image of Trilateralist thought and practice.

FOOTNOTES CHAPTER 9

1. Garret FitzGerald, *"Political Cooperation: Towards a Common EEC Foreign Policy"*, Commission of the European Communities,European Community, September-October 1978, p. 18.

2. Ibid., p. 20.

3. *Aspen Institute of Berlin Catalogue*, p. 2.

4. Ibid., p. 2.

5. Ibid., p. 3.

CHAPTER TEN

CONCLUDING THOUGHTS

There is no doubt that the Trilateral Commission exists: it is not a figment of a wild imagination as some of its supporters claim. Further, this Commission has written policies and set objectives. During the Carter administration, members of the Commission had the majority of executive branch power under their control, and it doesn't look like much is changing under the new Reagan administration.

At this point, it is useful to address the criticism of the Trilateral Commission, and the counter-criticism from the Commission itself.

David Rockefeller's feelings about Trilateral critics have been amply demonstrated: he views himself as the "moderate middle," and puts his critics on the "far right." This same theme was used in the November 24, 1980 issue of *Forbes Magazine*: Washington Bureau Chief Jerry Flint titled his article *What's a Trilateral Commission?* and captioned it "Why Marxists and Birchers love to hate the Trilateral Commission."[1]

Flint stated,

"On the Right radical end of the political fringe, for example, is Patrick Wood, co-author of the book Trilaterals Over Washington — 53,000 sold, he says —

*ias a new expose coming and who publishes a
hly newsletter, The Trilateral Observer, from
tsdale, Ariz. He warns that the Trilaterals want to
ເ̲ e America's economic independence for some kind
of new, world economic order, a playground for the
multinationals, manipulating governments for their
profits."[2]*

The article then talked about the John Birch Society (right-
wing), Laurence Shoup (a Marxist writer) and *Penthouse*
magazine. Flint interviewed Commission coordinator and
member **George Franklin** who claimed "We haven't a single
advocate of world government . . ."[3]

One of Flint's concluding thoughts was "Alas, people and
their conspiracy theories are not easily parted. It is much easier
to imagine a villain than to think things through."[4]

When this coauthor (Wood) was interviewed, Flint was
pointedly told that neither Sutton nor Wood advocate, teach or
believe in a "conspiracy" theory as such. This position has been
expounded on dozens of radio and TV shows all over America,
and on numerous of prestigious speaking platforms.

A conspiracy is defined by Webster's as "a secret agreement to
do something legal or illegal." Since the coauthors have had
little trouble in acquiring information on Trilateral activities
and positions, it can hardly be called a secret organizaion.
Further, who has a right to act as judge and jury to determine
legality or illegality of specific acts by members of the Trilateral
Commission? (This requires a Congressional investigation into
the facts presented in *Trilaterals Over Washington*.)

The Forbes article is significant for the following reasons:

- Flint ignored the reasons given for the coauthors'
  refusal to be involved with "conspiracy" tactics.
- He arbitrarily placed the authors in the "Right radical
  end of the political fringe," implied to be even to the
  right of the John Birch Society.
- He *did not mention* Professor Antony Sutton's name
  anywhere in the article, nor the fact that he was formerly
  a research fellow with Hoover Institution for War,
  Peace and Revolution at Stanford University — hardly

the "Right radical end" of anything!

- Ignored was *The Nation's* recent article attacking the Trilateral Commission. *The Nation* is one of the most presigous *liberal* publications in the country.[5]
- Also ignored was the suppressed criticism of the Commission by Nobel Laureate Professor George Wald in August 1980[6] — the reader may not agree with the criticism, but certainly cannot discount the source and the platform.[7]

The *Forbes* article typifies "establishment" handling of critics of the Commission. Responsible and researched criticism is "associated" with various minority radical elements in the country.

Since the truth of the matter (the facts) cannot be discredited, they attempt to discredit the critic. This is a shallow and weak ploy, not too difficult to see through.

To be fair though, some credit can be given the Commission in sending representatives to participate in public debates around the US with the coauthors. North American Secretary Charles Heck appeared with Patrick Wood on the nationally broadcasted *Larry King Show* on the Mutual Broadcasting System, among others. Commissioners **George Franklin** and **Phillip Trezise** debated with Antony Sutton at different times. **George Franklin** has debated with left-wing Trilateral critic Howard Katz on an influential T.V. program in Florida.

It is the personal experience of the authors that when public response was measured (i.e., on "call-in" radio, T.V. shows or public speaking events), sentiment was at least 95% hostile to the position of the Trilateral Commission and only 5% against the position taken by the coauthors. While Commission members have no reason to admit it, overwhelming public antipathy against the Commission has stung deeply.

It has never been the coauthors' intent to unfairly discredit a a person in contrast to the philosophy that person holds. People are people but ideas differ. When facts don't line up with a person's philosophy, and this discrepancy is pointed out, it is difficult for the person to resolve the discrepancy. The reaction will most likely be negative, ranging from ignoring the facts to lashing out at the person(s) delivering the facts.

The coauthors readily admit that a certain amount of their own bias shows in their writings, but this is only natural. Despite this, these works have been used by both conservative and liberal writers around the world. The reason is the coauthors' integrity for reporting facts is unquestioned, even if the reader disagrees with the conclusions offered.

As you have read this book, you may have arrived at different conclusions than the coauthors; in any case, you are probably antithetic to the Trilateral Commission and to the proposed *New Economic World Order*. You are urged to further your information gathering in your own community or sphere of influence. Share what you find with others, including the coauthors.

Freedom of the press is predicated on a free interchange of ideas and information. Any attempts to suppress either must be protested to the limit of moral restraint.

All in all, the information in this book (and in Volume I, as well) shows a very bleak picture of politics and the economics in the United States. Even so, it is a mistake to just abandon the field to the elite. God gave you a thinker (your brain) that is able to discern reality from fiction and fantasy; don't be swayed by psychological pressure designed to discredit what you think. Even if your thinking is *wrong*, if you let someone browbeat you out of your position, you will still be wrong. Test everything — weigh, digest, chew, mull over, check, research, etc.

Then stand on *your* findings and decisions.

Finally, the coauthors believe that once the American in the street realizes the full implications of the Trilateral process, then Trilateralism will receive outright rejection. The reason is simple: Trilateralism is diametrically opposed to the US Constitution and will ultimately require removal of the Constitution if the New Economic World Order is to succeed.

FOOTNOTES CHAPTER 10

1. Jerry Flint, *What's a Trilateral Commission?*, Forbes (November 24, 1980), p. 45.
2. Ibid., p. 45.
3. Ibid., p. 46.
4. Ibid., p. 49.

APPENDIX A

APPENDIX A

NEWS NOTES

1979

TREASURY GOLD SALES

Treasury gold sales seem to be reaching the bottom of the barrel — or the vaults. The 16 January 1979 Treasury gold sale consisted of 1,000,000 fine troy ounces of .995 to .999 and 500,000 fine troy ounces of .899 to .901. The latter is technically known as "coin melt," which is from gold coins seized by President Franklin D. Roosevelt in April 1933 from American citizens, or their heirs.

TRILATERALS IN IRAN

The December 23 issue of *La Lettre d'Information* written and published by Pierre de Villamarest in Paris, has a startling report, "Les Trilateralists et les liberaux de CFR facilitent le jeu de l'URSS en Iran." ("The Trilateralist and the CFR liberals facilitate the Soviet play in Iran.") This article supports the T.O. analysis that our Trilateral rulers may have played a double game in Iran. The new Iranian government has a former vice-president of Chase Manhattan Bank in the cabinet, and has already cut off oil to Israel and South Africa.

WHERE THE TRILATERALS THINK THEY ARE GOING

In late December, 1978, *New York Times* columnist James Reston interviewed the original executive director of the Trilateral Commission Zbigniew Brzezinski, who is now chairman of the National Security Council. Here are some **Brzezinski** highlights:

> *". . . we are engaged in shaping a genuine framework for cooperation for a world that, for the first time in history, has become politically active and awakened.*
>
> *I think the most fundamental force of change in our time is the massive awakening of man politically and socially."*

Comment: Note the emphasis on political power. The **Kissinger-Brzezinski** power politics approach has historically always led to war.

> *"It will take some time for a shared perspective to emerge. One of the things which President Carter has done, I think, is to begin to reestablish confidence in our institutions and confidence in our role in the world."*
>
> *"Chief U.S. Delegate. to the United Nations Andy Young has been a very constructive force in the United Nations."*
>
> *"We have had setbacks. We have not managed to bring the world economy under more effective control."*
>
> *". . . The Whites in southern Africa have been utterly unyielding."*

In brief: What *Brzezinski* and his fellow Commissioners want is a world politically controllable, where everyone else is in error and only Trilateralists are right. *Brzezinski's* replies to James Reston have the earmarks of authoritarianism. Warning enough!

THE FRIENDS AND ENEMIES OF TRILATERALISM

The Freedom House 1978 survey of political and civil rights in various countries sheds some remarkable light on Trilateral policy and double standard on human rights. Freedom House groups countries as "free," "partly free," and "not free."

Which are the Trilateralist favored countries? The "not free" countries include Communist China, Angola, the USSR and Zaire.

These are countries where Trilaterals want to forge "interdependence" or are kept afloat by US loans (Zaire) or oil royalties (Angola).

Trilateralist enemies in the "partly free" category include South Africa, Taiwan and Nicaragua.

The significance is this: if Trilateralism is associated with non-freedom now, then what will the global one-world "paradise" be like? Obviously it will be without civil and political liberties of any kind!

UPDATE ON WELLS FARGO BANK

Ernest C. Arbuckle is no longer a Trilateral Commissioner. This removes the representation of Wells Fargo. The only Wells Fargo link with Trilateralism is now very weak and insignificant, i.e., Continental Illinois Bank is the 10th largest shareholder in Wells Fargo.

It should also be noted that Wells Fargo is the first known corporation to give Proposition 13 tax savings for non-corporate purposes, mostly to public television and community aid agencies.

Further, **Arbuckle** is no longer with Wells Fargo — he is now chairman of the board of the Saga Corporation, a huge restaurant chain.

CENSORSHIP BY TRILATERALIST COOPER

A State Department business advisory committee known as the Advisory Committee on Transnational Enterprises contains top level corporate officials to advise the State Department on multinational matters.

Under Secretary of State for Economic Affairs **Richard N. Cooper** has imposed a requirement for security clearance on all public members of the Committee. It is difficult to see what relevance security clearances has for such topics as international accounting standards, code of ethics and transfer of technology to underdeveloped countries. The practical effect, however, is to prevent information from flowing to the business world at large and to keep the benefits of such information within a small group of multinationals.

THE WORLD OF CHASE

The new civilian government in Iran led by Prime Minister Shahpur Bakhtiar will no longer ship oil to South Africa and Israel. Iran had long been South Africa's major supplier, and supplied about 80% of the oil requirements of both countries.

The new minister of Economic and Finance Affairs is Rostam Pirasteh, a former vice president of Chase Manhattan Bank.

JUDGED BY THE COMPANY ONE KEEPS

Kevin Lynch reports (*National Review Bulletin,* 29 December 1978) that back in 1971, Trilateral **Andrew Young** attended a Gulf Oil stockholder meeting and nominated four persons as directors: **Andrew Young,** Angela Davis, Amilcar Cabral (an African Marxist now in the Guinea-Bissau government) and Agostinho Neto, the present Marxist dictator of Angola.

Lynch omitted to report, however, that today Gulf Oil is Neto's biggest financial backer and its operations are defended by Marxist forces. Things could hardly have been different if Young and his friends had been voted directors.

CARTER EDUCATION PHILOSOPHY

Assistant Secretary of State for Education Mary F. Berry visited the People's Republic of China. In a speech delivered at the University of Illinois on November 17, 1977, Berry recorded her favorable views of Communist Chinese education and the applicability of these ideas to the United States. For example:

> *". . . we do intend to work more aggressively to implement a realistic education and work strategy — one that in the context of American culture and a capitalistic economy addresses the basic problem of aliention of workers from their labor. We will draw on the Chinese model in our work."*

> *". . . I have shared with you today the view I received of our Chinese counterparts. Their experience may not,*

in every instance, be directly applicable here. But the direction of their overall policy - terms of access to education as well as of redefinition of education as something inextricably linked to the other aspects of human life — should, I believe, represent our basic direction also."

NEW YORK MONEY CENTER

The following article, reproduced in full, appeared in the *San Francisco Chronicle* on December 25, 1978:

"The Carter administration, throwing its support behind an economic development priority of New York Governor Hugh L. Carey, has quietly endorsed a controversial proposal to establish a 'free trade zone' for international banking activity in New York City.

"In a free trade zone, banks based in New York City would be able to conduct international operations unencumbered by state and city taxes or by Federal Reserve Board requirements and interest-rate ceilings. Carey and the banks say such a move would lure billions of dollars worth of bank activity back to the city from havens overseas, thus creating 5,000 to 6,000 local jobs. However, Federal Reserve Board approval is required, and the board is known to have serious misgivings. There is also outspoken opposition among some in Congress, who fear it would drastically increase unregulated banking activity at a time when they say regulations of banks should be tightened.

"In a letter to G. William Miller, chairman of the Federal Reserve, Robert Carswell, deputy secretary of the Treasury, gave a qualified endorsement to the concept of a free trade zone provided certain regulatory questions can be resolved. The Fed has invited comment on the idea before it makes a final decision on the proposal next year.

"If the Fed approved a free trade zone, international banking activity would be exempt from US regulations.

"Many experts fear that large corporate depositors in

the United States could then shift their deposits from domestic branches into the 'international branches' of the banks. This would, in turn, create a large amount of money flowing into an unregualted sector of the banking industry.

"In addition, foreign deposits in United States banks - now estimated by the Federal Reserve at more than $20 billion - might also flow into the international zone."

The implications of such a move hardly require explanation here!

DOUBLE TAKE

Many otherwise well-informed Americans have resisted the evidence of a link between world imperialism (represented by the multinationals and the US elite) with world communism. *The Wall Street Journal* (15 February 1979) ran a news item: *Business That Financed "Das Kapital" is Folding More than 100 years after Karl Marx wrote "Das Kapital."*

The news item reports that the German textile firm of Ermen & Engels has been sold and Braunswerth Palace, the Engels family mansion, will be demolished.

Fredrich Engels, of course, used the family fortune to finance Karl Marx and his family in London while Marx wrote the books that revolutionized the world.

The Wall Street Journal could have added other pertinent details of the cozy relationship between capitalism and communism. For example, the protection given by the British Home Office to Karl Marx while he was in London and Marx's friendship with members of the British establishment. The latter evolved into the Atlantic Alliance known as the Council on Foreign Relations. One day perhaps this history, presently unknown, will see the light of day.

WILLIAM E. BROCK III

William E. Brock, III is a Trilateral Commissioner, and a member of the CFR. He is also chairman of the Republican

National Committee and is in a key position to influence the Republican Party towards a Trilaterist One World economy.

A key instance of this influence is in the promotion of the International Year of the Child, promoted around the world by socialists, communists and Trilateralists. (See *Trilateral Observer,* February 1979)

The Republican Study Committee in the House of Representatives has blasted the International Year of the Child along the lines reported by T.O. — however, true to Trilateral form, **Brock** is promoting Jesse Jackson, a prominent member of the US Commission on the IYC. Further, the *Wall Street Journal* reports Brock as "eagerly courting" Jackson.

TRILATERAL DOUBLE TALK

Governor **James Thompson** of Illinois has pronounced that "as of now he does not intend to run for the Presidency in 1980." But *The Washington Star* makes the following comment:

> *"The statement is not a pledge to serve out his present four-year term which has just started. It is not a pledge, he said, that is my intention."*

Thompson is still very much a Trilateral candidate for 1980.

CARNEGIE ENDOWMENT

Trilateralist **Thomas L. Hughes** is president of the Carnegie Endowment. The Carnegie Commission on the Future of Public Broadcasting has issued a long awaited report. It proposes, among other things: use of $1.2 billion a year of public tax funds, a centralized Public Telecommunications Trust (PTT), a single source of national programming and extension into full-service programming.

The present Public Broadcasting System is localized — some 170 licensees operate 270 completely independent local public television stations. The Carnegie Commission not unexpectedly wants centralization, in line with Trilateral objectives of central control.

INTERNAL REVENUE SERVICE

The IRS, swamped by increasing tax protests, has decided to use "criminal sanctions against the promoters of tax protest schemes."

This will be an excellent opportunity for a First Amendment challenge to the IRS (shades of King George III!).

Does the IRS believe that criminal sanctions will stop a protest? All it will do is escalate the struggle. We shall see the day when IRS agents will have to disguise their occupation, even from friends, and IRS offices will be barred, guarded and shuttered.

CATO INSTITUTE

TO readers should be aware of the Anthony Harrigan column, **Cato and the New Left.** The San Francisco-based Cato Institute is supposedly based on libertarian free market principles.

However, the Institute has developed over a period of time a relationship with the Institute for Policy Studies in Washington, D.C., whose subsidiary is the Transnational Institute. The latter has international Marxist connections - a long way from libertarian principles. (For the complete report write Anthony Harrigan, Home Federal Building, Nashville, Tennessee 37219.)

ROCKEFELLER INTERVIEW

The February 24, 1979 issue of the *San Francisco Chronicle* reported on a personal interview with **David Rockefeller,** who was there checking up on some business interests. (See p. 44, Business World section, Donald K. White, Business Editor.) The hypocrisy of **Rockefeller's** statements is astounding:

> *"Taking an ask me anything attitude and without the back-up team of experts that most top bankers and industrialists bring with them,* **Rockefeller** *said that he expects the U.S. economy to go through a shallow recession before 1979 is out.*

> *"He also said that he expects the Iranian government to pay that country's debts to U.S. banks, including a reported $200 million owed to Chase Manhattan.* Ed: What does **Rockefeller** know that we don't know?

> *"***Rockefeller** *is against a proposed constitutional*

convention that would prohibit U.S. deficits and he thinks government regulations are having a serious impact on U.S. productivity.

"**Rockefeller** *was particularly critical of Jimmy Carter's use of human rights policies in foreign countries as a reason for economic sanctions.*

" '*In my view,' he said, 'the belief that trade can be an effective instrument to influence the social and environmental policies of other nations is ill-conceived, misguided and often counter productive. Repeated lecturing and public condemnation of regimes that we find repressive are not likely to produce the desired results...*

" '... *Our attitude is viewed by many as self-righteous and offensive.'*

"*In the international trade arena,* **Rockefeller** *said, 'U.S. businessmen are too reluctant to play the game.'* "

MULTINATIONAL PROFITS AND TAXES

The Washington Post (March 5, 1979) reports a Treasury Department spokesman as making the following statement:

"The global operations of U.S. multinational companies complicate the task of tax collectors and regulators.

"Current U.S. tax law permits deferral of American taxes on most income left abroad, allowing companies to shelter their profits in European banks or foreign bonds.

"Very little U.S. tax revenue is collected on income of U.S. foreign subsidiaries."

We have argued several times in TO that Trilateral multinationals adopt the above-cited policies to the detriment of the United States. It's good to have official Treasury confirmation.

FROM CALIFORNIA STATE PRISONS

This news item is only tangentially related to Trilateralism, but we like it anyway.

Last December there was a block in Vacaville State Prison in California which had the following inmates in adjacent cells:

- Will Spann, (robbery) nephew of Trilateral **Jimmy Carter**
- Charles Manson
- Michael Dellums, son of Congressman Ronald Dellums who has just replaced Congressman Diggs on the House District Committee

Michael Dellums was released in December but is now back in an Oakland California jail — charged with murder.

ANOTHER TRILATERAL BANK HEADS FOR CHINA

The Bank of America is right on the heels of Chase Manhattan for the Communist China business.

Two Trilaterals are on the board of parent BankAmerica Corporation (**Clausen** and **Wood**).

Clausen was recently in Peking. We note the following:

- **Clausen** received royal treatment including a special chauffeured car.
- The deal involves a $1 billion B of A loan to Red China.
- B of A has been invited to establish an office in Peking.
- **Clausen** considers China to be "eminently credit worthy."

It will be interesting to record the interest rate on this loan. It will certainly be less than paid by US business firms to B of A.

Remember B of A made a contribution of $25,000.00 to defeat California's Proposition 13.

FRENCH ELITISM

La Lettre d'Information edited by Perre de Villemarest (C.E.I. La Vendomierre, 27930 Le Cierrey, France — 400 Francs per year) reports the following on Trilateral **Thierry De Montbrial**: (Our translation)

> *"Since 1978 among the 26 members of the directors' committee of the Bilderbergers is a single Frenchman Thierry de Montbrial, also a Trilateral. Montbrial became, in January 1979, secretary - general of*

L'Institut Francais des Relations Internationales formerly Center de Politique Etrangere, an elitist group which hides behind its seminars and publications direct links with the American CFR and the Soviets in the East."

Thierry De Montbrial is a professor of economics at the Ecole Polytechnique in Paris.

REPUBLICAN PAUL FINDLEY

Republican Paul Findley is not a Trilaterist but is a perennial sponsor of the Atlantic Union bill. Our last issue touched on the links between Trilateralism and the Atlantic Union.

At a luncheon for Han Xu (Chinese People's Republic liaison in Washington, D.C.) Paul Findley was garbed in a large Maoist coat decorated with a small American flag.

We trust this does not reflect the proportions of the Congressman's allegiance. (Photograph in *Washington Star,* February 9, 1979)

ENERGY: THE CREATED CRISIS

Consider the following:

The U.S. has an 80 million gallon underground reserve of oil — but no pumps to get the oil back out of the ground. It was planned that way according to the *Wall Street Journal,* March 15, 1979.

The **Carter** Administration has halted power production by five of the largest nuclear plants. The excuse is a computer error — identified as far back as 1972.

Department of Energy claims the Iranian cutoff has created a world shortage of 2.5 million barrels a day. Senator Gore cites a Congressional study to the effect the shortage is a mere 80,000 barrels a day, because of increased output elsewhere. (Anyway, the Iranians are back in production and shipping oil.)

Exxon diverted a shipment of Venezuelan oil to New England from its original Canadian destination. The oil was sold at the high spot price. Next day Venezuela increased the price of all its oil by the same percentage. Who controls Exxon? Enough said?

DIE ZEIT AGAIN

Rapid deployment of the Soviet SS-20 poses a major threat to West Germany. Responsible authorities in Germany propose that the United States deploy Pershing II missles in that country as a warning to the Soviets.

The opposition to the idea? From none other than *Die Zeit* with Trilateralist **Theo Sommer** as editor-in-chief.

If Trilateralist policy is to abandon West Germany then this should be made known to Germans in general.

FINANCIAL WORLD TO THE RESCUE

We have recounted the role of Boeing Company (**T. Wilson** is President) in conveying top secret data to the Soviet Union.

The March 15, 1979 issue of *Financial World* comes to the aid of **Wilson** by naming him "Chief Executive Officer of the Year" with a front page color photograph and a glowing article on **Wilson's** achievements.

Not one word on the Boeing espionage scandal, however.

THE VALUE ADDED TAX

The idea of value added tax has surfaced again. The bait is reduction in the income tax. Presumably some will take the bait but most US citizens will conclude that if we have a VAT then the income tax will stay as well on some phony ground or another.

Trilateral **W. Michael Blumenthal** has declared he is "not unsympathetic" to VAT which is also being promoted by Senator Russell B. Long, chairman of the Senate Finance Committee.

If ever a proposal needs to be shot down fast, it is VAT.

UPDATE ON EUROPEAN TRILATERALISM

Italian Trilaterals have again demonstrated how Trilaterals use the political power of the state, in this case the Italian state, to advance their own interests.

The Italian government is in final stages of negotiating of $1 billion line of credit for Communist China. The interest rates will be 7¼% for the first five years and 7½% for the remaining years, for an eight year credit line.

Who will receive the benefit of these credits? Small and medium-sized Italian companies, or even large Italian companies? Not at all. The "new China policy" is a Trilateral policy and so the bulk of the Italian credit line will go to the Trilateralists. Fiat S.p.A. (president is **Giovanni Agnelli,** member of the executive board of the Trilateral Commission) has a $600 million deal to build an agricultural machinery plant in China: that accounts for 60% of the $1 billion Italian loan right there. Montedison, a large Italian chemical complex, is represented by Trilateralist **Umberto Columbo,** director general of Montedison's Research and Development Division. This company is negotiating three plants worth about $200 million -- that's another 20% of the $1 billion loan. In brief: two Trilateral firms already have the bulk of an official Italian Government loan earmarked for their own interests.

ON SUING BUREAUCRATS

The *London Daily Telegraph* has filed suit against the (British) Price Commission for $15,700.00 to cover 948 man hours spent in digging out information demanded by bureaucrats.

Not surprisingly The *Financial Times* of London (Trilateralis **Ferdy Fisher** is editor) is unsympathetic to this move calling the *Daily Telegraph* "archconservative," following the Trilateral tradition of occupying the center ground and calling everyone else "extremist" of either the right or the left.

Suing the state might be a worthwhile tactic for US companies to follow.

HOW THEY DO IT

How did Joan Mondale, wife of Trilateral **Walter Mondale** (vice president of the United States) become the art expert of the **Carter** administration? According to UPI her explanation is: "After the election somebody came up to me and said 'Rosalynn Carter's going to do mental health, what are you going to do?' "

TRILATERALS IN HOLLAND

Holland has three (3) Trilateral representatives including **Th. M. Scholten,** chairman of the Robeco Investment Group. We include **Scholten** as part of the Trilateral power base because of the Robeco financial interests.

The multinational ramifications of Robeco are of interest because they demonstrate that some non-US multinationals are very much part of the creation of a New Economic World Order under multinational control.

Robeco has about $5 billion in assets, the largest investment group in Europe. Its property holding subsidiary has 45% of its investments in the US, 38% in Holland and the remainder in Belgium, West Germany and France.

In brief, Robeco is evidence that Trilateralism is not a purely American phenomenon. It is a power group created by a group of internationalists for particular purposes. National identification is a temporary label. The common ground between **David Rockefeller, Giovanni Agnelli** and **Th. M. Scholten** is that they have no national allegiances. They see the world as a single entity and world politics as a device to divert the world's resources to their own profit.

TRILATERALS AND BILDERBERGERS

Pierre de Villemarest of France has published the interlocks between Trilaterals, CFR and Bilderbergers.

The International Executive Committee of the Bilderbergers has twenty-six (26) members, of which eleven, or 46% of the total, are Trilaterals:

Th. de Montbrial (France)
Theo Sommer (West Germany)
Otto Wolff von Amerongen (West Germany)
Max Kohnstamm (Italy)
Otto Grieg Tidemand (Norway)
Lord Roll (United Kingdom)
George W. Ball (United States)
David Rockefeller (United States)
Arthur R. Taylor (United States)
Henry Kissinger (United States)

ENERGY: THE CREATED CRISIS

TO readers may only be a relatively small subgroup of the United States population, but apparently their views are widely held.

Channel 4 TV in San Francisco took a poll of its viewers on March 27 with the question, "Have oil companies contrived the oil and gas shortage?"

An overwhelming *Yes* vote came in with 2,274; those who said *No* only numbered 215!

SALT II CANNOT BE VERIFIED

The **Carter** Administration is pulling out all stops to suppress discussion of Salt II, and for good reason — no verification is possible.

A speech by Senator **John Glenn** (also a Trilateral) was censored by **Glenn** himself after consultation with fellow Trilateral **Carter**. No fewer than eleven (11) paragraphs were deleted on the grounds they were too sensitive for "public discussion." (Associated Press, April 8) Regrettably **Glenn** is chairman of the Senate Subcommittee that oversees nuclear proliferation.

Says General Daniel Graham, former head of the U.S. Defense Intelligence Agency, "With the loss of our important bases in Iran, we no longer have the facilities nor capability to monitor or verify Salt I, much less Salt II."

For more information contact: Citizens for Better Government, P.O. Box 16483, Lubbock, Texas 79490.

THE LONG ARM OF TRILATERALISM

We have always suspected that Trilaterals have a pervasive influence in the media — but not quite to the extent recently reported to TO from England.

Apparently members of the Liberal Party in Bristol, England, ("liberal" over there includes "dismantling the state apparatus where it restricts or wastes," unlike totalitarian liberalism in the US) placed an advertisement in the local newspaper calling public attention to the Trilateral Commission.

The Bristol newspaper took upon itself to subtly, yet

effectively, change the advertisement by inserting a question mark in a crucial place so that the copy read as follows:

"M.H. Ferdy Fisher (a Trilateral Commission member?)"

We have commented before on the weak knees of those like the *Conservative Digest* who refuse to even accept advertisements naming the Trilateral Commission, but this British newspaper has gone one step further: it takes the advertiser's money and then distorts the ad!

Unfortunately for these eager-beaver censors, history records that censorship in any form never succeeds. Hitler and Stalin are witnesses to this axiom.

THE MAKING OF MR. CARTER

H du B Reports has published an interesting account of the mechanism by which **Jimmy Carter** was selected and "sold" to the American people. The report includes such well-known names as Averell Harriman, Milton Katz, General Paul Stehlen, **Zbigniew Brzezinski** and **David Rockefeller.** It has interesting information that this editor has not seen published elsewhere. (Send $1.00 and ask for *The Making of a President* to H du B Reports, P.O. Box 786, St. George, Utah 84770.)

RHODESIA

The pro-Marxist stance of the Trilateral administration in Washington was dramatically emphasized by its negative attitude to Rhodesian elections and the new black majority government.

Washington refused to send election observers on the grounds that the Marxist terrorists — presently attempting to destroy Rhodesia — were not running the show. When a black majority government was elected — with a more that 60% turnout — Washington still dragged its heels.

Bishop Abel Muzorewa, the new black Rhodesian Prime Minister-elect, says he will accept South African military aid.

In brief: Trilaterals in Washington are not interested in human rights or black rights — but merely the right to support totalitarian governments on the road to New Economic World Order.

BOEING COMPANY — AGAIN

The Federal Trade Commission has accused Boeing Company of illegal bribes amounting to about $5 million given to foreign officials to influence purchasing decisions in favor of Boeing. (We reported recently that Boeing Company — Trilateral **T.A. Wilson** is chairman of the board—was involved in Soviet espionage with the "X" Missile.)

Comments Boeing:

"We have always refused to concede that the name— bribery — could be associated with any of our activities." Boeing wants to call the illegal payments "fees" or "commissions."

Unfortunately, Boeing filed a sworn affidavit with Justice Department asserting it had paid no fees or commissions in these instances.

TRILATERAL HENRY KISSINGER

Kissinger is still making news in the establishment media.

In mid-April **Kissinger** spent three days in Tokyo and Japan to attend the Trilateral "private summit." Topics discussed included:

- energy
- the China policy
- international financial stability
- trade and balance of payments problems

Kissinger also argued for a greater Japanese military effort.

On the domestic front, **Kissinger** is attempting to block public access to telephone conversations made while national security advisor and secretary of state. Although the notes were made by aides paid by the US government (i.e., the taxpayer), **Kissinger** argues they are his personal property and not subject to public disclosure.

Several of the recorded conversations were leaked by Jack Anderson including the following conversation with Ambassador Black:

Kissinger: *"Twelve days in Africa will drive me to drink. I have yet to meet a foreign minister with whom I have more than 45 minutes of real conversation."*

Black: *"I think you would have no trouble talking to Ghanians. Foreign Minister Felli is a most interesting man."*

Kissinger: *"Boredom is not a problem. The question is how to cover all these countries."*

Black: *"Come on the 23rd. It is my birthday."*

Kissinger: *"You are a Taurus."*

Black: *"That is why I am so pushy."*

Kissinger: *"I am a Gemini. That means I am two-faced."*

TRILATERALIST JOHN GLENN

We reported last month that under White House pressure Senator **John Glenn** has censored his comments on the new Salt II pact. Apparently **Glenn** has now loosened the censorship and on CBS "Face the Nation" warned that Soviet compliance cannot be verified and that it is unlikely that the Senate will approve the treaty unless the administration provides assurances of verification.

The point to note is that compliance cannot be certified and any "assurances" will be phony for public consumption, we shall watch to see if Trilateralist **John Glenn** holds his position or buckles under White House pressure again.

COMPUTERS FOR THE SOVIETS

In July, 1978, **Jimmy Carter** made a great publicity splash in denying export of a $6.8 million Sperry Univac computer to the Soviet Union. The Soviets said they wanted it for their news agency Tass to help cover the 1980 Olympics in Moscow. The White House said it was too powerful for the stated purpose.

Now a Honeywell subsidiary, CII-Honeywell Bull of France has sold a similar computer to the Soviets which will perform the same functions as the banned computer. This French company is 47% owned by Honeywell of the United States.

The mystery is this: Sperry Rand has no Trilateral representation and as of this month thinks it has "a valid contract with the Soviets" for the Tass computer.

However, Honeywell, Inc. has Trilateral representation in the shape of Commissioner **Edson W. Spencer,** president and chief executive officer.

Spencer is a former Rhodes scholar and director of the Council on Foreign Relations.

Could it be that the White House blocks the sale of the Sperry computer last year to make way for a Honeywell computer?

LEONARD WOODCOCK ON CHINA

Leonard Woodcock, US Ambassador to China, was listed as a Trilateralist in the early membership rosters but not in more recent lists. As in the case of **George Bush,** we prefer to assume that Trilateral ideas and influence continue in **Woodcock's** work.

Leonard Woodcock was formerly president of the United Auto Worker's Union and before that a member of the US Socialist Party. **Woodcock's** father was associated with Sidney and Beatrice Webb, founders of the socialist Fabian Society and the London School of Economics. **Woodcock** collaborated with Walter Reuther in 1962 to fund and found the Students for a Democratic Society. More recently, **Woodcock** was a member of the executive board of Common Cause, an establishment vehicle to promote ideas and policies useful to a one world authoritarian society.

In early May, 1979, **Woodcock** was in New York and addressed a meeting of the Asia Society. Among his points were several that highlight the extraordinary parallel between the ongoing build-up of Communist China by Wall Street and the similar technical build up of Communist Russia in the early 1920's by the same banks and major corporations (or their descendents) **Woodcock** made the following observations:

- China will be forming joint ventures and stock companies with foreign partners. This is similar to the several hundred joint stock companies established by the USSR and foreign companies (Fiat, Ford, Chase, General Electric, Westinghouse, International Harvester, etc.) in the early 1920's.

- China wants older technology, not super-sophisticated computerized technology.
- China needs to upgrade capacity already in place (the same task undertaken by US and German companies in 1920's Russia).
- China's largest source of currency to buy this technology will be "oil, nonferrous metals and coal." (In 1920's Russia's source of foreign exchange was oil, gold and nonferrous metals.)
- Woodcock predicted that China will join the World Bank and the International Monetary Fund.
- Finally, Woodcock suggested that China's external debt could reach $20 billion by 1985.

CHASE MANHATTAN AND CHINA

At this time only Chase Manhattan has put together a loan for Communist China. It has made available $50 million for construction of a foreign trade building in Peking and will arrange syndicate financing for the balance of $200 million.

PETRO CANADA

Petro Canada is the Canadian government oil company with $2.5 billion in assets and under fire in Canada for its attempted take over of the Canadian oil industry.

Maurice F. Strong, chairman of Petro Canada is no longer listed as a Trilateral Commissioner, but has been replaced in the Commission by its deputy chairman, **Donald Southam Harvie.**

Legislation now pending in the Canadian legislature would give Petro Canada 35% of all new oil exploration ventures. However, upcoming elections pose a threat to its existence. The Canadian Conservative Party intends to denationalize Petro Canada on the grounds it is a waste of public funds. "Petro

Canada has not found one barrel of oil on its own" says Joe Clark, leader of Canadian conservatives. Trilateral support for nationalization and government corporations is a clear indicator of its long range intentions to convert the world into a complex of state-run corporations with Trilaterals pulling the political strings.

CONTINENTAL ILLINOIS BANK

Continental Illinois is the nation's seventh largest bank — holding company — an aggressive and pushy bank operation.

Three Trilateral Commissioners are on the board of directors: **Hewitt, Perkins and Wood.**

In 1978, Continental loans expanded by 28% (compared to an average 17% for large banks). Its earnings jumped 17% compared to 12% for the average large bank.

Says one of its competitors: "We hear that Continental is willing to do just about anything to make a deal."

On the other hand, the bank is running out of steam. Says one observer: "The wind is going out of Continental's sails and because the bank is rapidly burning up its capital base, it has had to come to the market for equity, and it will have to keep coming, leading to dilution of the capital base."

COCA-COLA

Coca-Cola's Minute Maid division has the monopoly to supply orange juice to the 1980 Moscow Olympics. Enthused, a spokesman for Coca-Cola, "The P.R. possibilities are truly legion." **J. Paul Austin,** Trilateral Commissioner and **Carter** backer, is chairman of the Coca-Cola Company.

Maybe we should switch our orange juice purchases at the local supermarket away from Minute Maid into some other brands?

THE WALL STREET JOURNAL

The Wall Street Journal is an excellent source of current news: we read it every day.

However, even the august *Wall Street Journal* is required to conceal the activities of Trilaterals. We can arrive at no other conclusion after a recent letter from Frederick Taylor (executive editor of the *WSJ*) to a TO reader, which has been made available to us.

The TO reader, a former NBC newsman, wrote Taylor to ask the following:

"You *never* mention David Rockefeller's Trilateral Commission, though knowledgeable people hold it to be the *de facto* foreign and domestic policy making[sic] body for the U.S. Jimmy Carter is its creature."

The reader added that this constitutes "slack journalism" and that The *Wall Street Journal* lacks completeness.

Frederick Taylor replied, "The knowledgeable people I know think the Trilateral Commission has about as much clout as the Chamber of Commerce."

Of course, any issue of *Trilateral Observer* will demolish Taylor's statement. We are left with two explanations for Taylor's "blind eye":

(1) Taylor honestly doesn't know about the Trilateral Commission and asked a Commissioner that he happened to know for an explanation. Of course, the supposed individual would give a whitewash answer. (This editor received similar whitewash answers from initial inquiries to CFR members in the late 1960's.)

(2) Taylor may be aware of the Trilateral Commission, but is unable to run news of its doings. We know that **J. Paul Austin** is a member of the board of Dow Jones & Co., Inc. We also conceive that a few words from **Austin** could soothe any doubts that Taylor might have about the Trilateral Commission.

We do not know *why* Taylor wants to submerge news about Trilateralism. Perhaps other interested readers of TO might take up arms and persuade Taylor that he is in error. *The Wall Street Journal* is too valuable a newspaper to be guilty of incompleteness.

THE NEWS CONCEALERS

TO will begin to list those publications willing to acknowledge the existence of Trilateral Commission — and the more flagrant concealers of their existence. In this way readers may judge who, in the media world, is willing to stand up and be counted and who is tacitly supporting a Trilateral takeover by silence.

As we reported above, *The Wall Street Journal* so far has its editorial and news head in the sand — it does not recognize the existence of the Trilateral Commission as a power force.

The Dines Letter (June 8, 1979) reports critically on the Trilateral attempt to infiltrate business with "worker participation."

ANDREW YOUNG

Recent weeks have seen a flurry of news items about Trilateralist **Andrew Young**, US Ambassador to the United Nations.

- *On NBC's Meet the Press* **Andrew Young** opposed lifting sanctions against Zimbabwe Rhodesia. As the new government is black, this exposes Trilateralist concealment of pro-Marxist objectives behind a screen of racism.

- *The New York Post* reports **Andrew Young** wants to quit his post as United Nations Ambassador and run for the Senate from Georgia. Also, it is reported that a successor to **Young** at the UN would be another Trilateral — **Richard Gardner,** now U.S. Ambassador to Italy.

- **Young** has made some asinine comments on the Spenkelink murder case (Spenkelink was executed in Florida).
  "I do not see any difference in the so-called due process in Florida and the so-called due process of the (Ayatollah) Khomeini."

In fact, the Spenkelink case went four times to the Florida Supreme Court, three times to the US Court of Appeals and five times to the US Supreme Court.

TRILATERAL AT GM

The 5/14/79 issue of *Automotive News* reports that **Dr.**

Marina von Neumann Whitman, age 44, was appointed vice president and chief economist for the huge auto-maker. She is also the second woman vice-president at GM.

The article states: "Whitman was a member of President Nixon's Council of Economic Advisers. She will join GM upon completion of a research sabbatical at the Center for Advanced Study in Behavioral Sciences at Stanford, California."

It appears that Stanford has indeed become a Trilateral think tank. What we can't quite figure out is how **Whitman** will use her newly found research in behavioral sciences!

JACK ANDERSON HITS NERVE

This column appeared in *The Washington Post* on June 20, 1979 — you figure it out! [Emphasis added.]

"Some fascinating documents, including a secret message from **Henry Kissinger** *to the Shah of Iran, have turned up in Washington. They were left behind by the Shah's urbane ambassador, Ardeshir Zahedi, after he vacated the Iranian Embassy.*

"The documents add some new jigsaw pieces to the great Iranian puzzle. They indicate that **Kissinger,** *after leaving government, continued to advise the Shah; that* **Kissinger** *recommended the return to prison of the dissidents whom President* **Carter** *had encouraged the Shah to release, and that* **Kissinger** *worked behind the scenes with the Rockefeller brothers, Nelson and* **David,** *to assist the Shah.*

"These startling allegations add to the puzzle that we have been piecing together from top-secret documents and exhaustive interviews. In past columns, we have established that the Rockefeller brothers had close financial ties to the Shah and that he had ordered his subordinates to channel Iranian oil funds through their Chase Manhattan Bank.

"Significantly, **Kissinger** *began his international career as a foreign policy director for the Rockefeller Brothers Fund. He is now back with the Rockefellers, at least nominally, as a consultant to the Chase Manhattan Bank.*

"*There is also suppressed, secret documentation that the Shah was the driving force behind the astronomical 500% leap in oil prices and that Saudi Arabia had offered to block the price rise in 1974 if the Nixon administration would intervene with the Shah. But* **Kissinger** *had stubbornly opposed any interference with the Shah, who was left free to continue agitating for higher prices.*

" *This persuaded the other oil-selling nations that the United States secretly supported the Shah's drive for the moon. Soon the oil billions began pouring into the Shah's coffers — much of it by way of the Chase Manhattan Bank.*

" *Banking sources in New York City, Paris and Geneva have told us that the Shah escaped with a staggering $25 billion, which he still controls through a maze of corporate fronts and bank accounts.*

"*In two interviews,* **Kissinger** *angrily denied the insinuation that his attitude toward the Shah was influenced in any way by the Rockefellers' financial dealings. His present services for the bank, he insisted, are strictly advisory. He also denied evidence that he has continued to advise and assist the Shah.*

"*But among the documents that the Shah's ambassador left behind in the Iranian Embassy were copies of cables he had sent to the Shah. One of them, classified top-secret and dated November 5, 1978, contains reactions to the Shah's decision to install military government.*

"*Translated from the Persian, the cable, written by Zahedi, begins with this salutation: "I kiss your feet thousands and thousands of times and beg you to allow me to report to His Imperial Majesty the following . .*

"*Among other tidbits, Zahedi reported: 'I talked to* **Kissinger** *at 6:30. He said he was glad to hear about the Shah's decisions and congratulations.' He also said, 'You have to stay young against all these critics. I believe that you have to get the prisoners you released earlier and put them in jail again. Your work will be easier if* *you put them in jail.'*

*"There was also a message from Nelson Rockefeller:
'I would like to convey to your Majesty my warmest
congratulations and respect for the courageous, wise
and statesmanlike decision which you have taken. By
this decision you have saved not only the West but also
Japan.'*

*"**Kissinger** told us that he made no such statement to
Zahedi; in fact, that he was out of town at the time.
Kissinger said it was not uncommon for ambassadors to
concoct false, flattering reports. It was also possible, he
suggested, for the Shah's enemies to have fabricated the
cable after they took over the embassy.*

*"We have also established that **Kissinger** and **David
Rockefeller,** chairman of the Chase Manhattan Bank,
made it their business to find a sanctuary for the
deposed Shah. Our sources say that **Rockefeller**
arranged the Shah's temporary refuge in Nassau and
that **Kissinger** intervened with President Jose Lopez
Portillo to get the Shah admitted to Mexico.*

*"Meanwhile, both **Kissinger** and **Rockefeller** tried in
vain to obtain permanent residence for the Shah in the
United States. **Rockefeller** also sent Robert Armao, a
former member of the late Nelson Rockefeller's vice-
presidential staff, to Nassau to coordinate the Shah's
operation.*

*"This curious Shah-**Rockefeller-Kissinger** connection appears to be in the center of the great Iranian
puzzle."*

TRILATERAL SUBVERSION

Evidence is surfacing that the Trilateralists are engaged in
extraordinary efforts to aid the Communist Chinese that can
only be described as subversive.

Washington Dateline reported (May 28, 1978, P.O. Box
40041, Washington, D.C., 20016) last year that Chinese
Communists had been allowed access to a top secret laser
research facility at University of Texas, Fort Davis, operating
under a U.S. Air Force contract. The press was not informed of

this visit.

This dovetails with the more recent Trilateral efforts to build up Communist military power with finance and technology, as reported in TO. This aspect of Trilateral activities needs careful watching. No doubt Trilateralists are convinced they are building a "one world." What Trilateralists do not understand, because it is a closed, self-perpetuating organization, is that Communists are adept at double-dealing. The kind of naive posturing typical of Trilateral writings suggest they are incapable of hard assessments of Communists' objectives.

TRILATERALIST NEWSPAPER IN THE US

The daily *Financial Times* of London, England is now printed in Frankfurt, West Germany for air mail distribution abroad. The European-American edition is flown to Kennedy Airport in New York and then shipped by jet to all parts of the United States, thus making a European newspaper available on date of publication in most major US cities.

However, we do not print this information with the suggestion you subscribe. The publicity blurb for the *Financial Times* begins:

"Never before has American business and *world* business been as interdependent." (Italics in original)

The key word is, of course, "interdependent," the password among one-world elitists.

The editor of *Financial Times* is none other than **Ferdy Fisher,** whom we discussed at some length in *Trilateral Censorship, The Case of C. Gordon Tether.* (TO, Vol. 1, No. 6, p. 46)

In brief: *The Financial Times* of London is becoming a world newspaper and will undoubtedly reflect one-world elitist ideas.

JEAN-LUC PEPIN

Canadian Trilateralist **Jean-Luc Pepin,** member of Parliament for the Carleton district of Ottawa, Canada was recently in Yugoslavia. **Pepin** was received by Jozo Bodruzic, presidnet of the so-called "parliament" of Bosnia-Herzegovina (a district in Yugoslavia). Reports are that they had a "long and warm" conversation.

HENRY KISSINGER

Former Secretary of State Trilateral Commissioner **Henry Kissinger** met recently in Peking with Hua Kuo-feng, Chinese Premier. This continues a series of unofficial meetings between Trilateralists and foreign heads of government.

RHODESIA

Foreign Affairs, the oracle of elitism, has announced failure to achieve a Marxist government in Rhodesia. In the summer 1979 issue, Richard H. Ullman writes on *Salvaging America's Rhodesian Policy.* Ullman suggests the US recognize that black leader Muzorewa has a viable government and that the old US policy is no longer useful. However, Ullman does not want trade sanctions lifted because he correctly assesses that Rhodesia would continue to look to South Africa. A key US objective is to break the Rhodesia-South Africa alliance.

Interestingly, Ullman admits the US has few cards left to play. Ullman does not, however, review a key issue — *that the US policy failed because elitist support of Marxist regimes is now crystal clear to many Americans and many overseas.*

CYRUS VANCE

Secretary of State and Trilateral Commissioner **Cyrus Vance** has come under attack in the French publication, *L'Express.* An article by Raymond Aron entitled (aptly), *The Serenity of Ostriches,* slashes the logic and intent of **Vance's** pronouncement on world affairs. Aron writes:

> *"One can't read such notions without fear and trembling. If the leaders of the American Republic must once again learn the nature and aspirations of the Soviet Union, then I fear that by the time the Secretary of State will have mastered the lesson there will be nothing left to defend."*

A recent speech by **Vance** in Chicago (May 1, 1979) emphasized the rather pitiful Trilateral meanderings which caused Arons' wrath. For example, **Vance** pronounced: "Let me share with you frankly my concern that the distorted proposition being advanced by some that America is in a period of decline in the world is not only wrong, as a matter of fact, but dangerous as a basis for policy." Yet later, **Vance** argues that we now are equal in armaments with the USSR and "only when both sides perceive a balance, as is now the case, can we hope for real arms control progress."

Then we find the cliche of "interdependence." "This growing economic interdependence requires that our government work with others to help create international conditions in which all nations can thrive." And much more of the same. Raymond Aron deserves our thanks.

ANOTHER TRILATERAL MEETING

In June 1979, **Michael Blumenthal, Henry Owen,** and the Trilateralist French Premier **Raymond Barre** met in Paris to discuss "global" energy and monetary problems.

FIRST NATIONAL BANK OF CHICAGO

The First National Bank of Chicago has significant Trilateral representation. First National has also become the first US bank to make a direct loan to China — $8 million to purchase coastal ships. According to the bank, Communist China is a "preferred creditor" in the world money market.

US CUSTOMS - FINALE

As if emphasizing our lead story this month, *The Rhoades Conclusion* (July 1979, $48.00 annually, P.O. Box 22674, San Diego, CA 92112) has printed the following news item:

"They're getting ready now. There are three bills in Congress designed to cut cash smuggling . . . in an attempt to curb the activity of narcotics dealers.

". . .One allows customs officials to search for cash without a court warrant; another pays up to $250,000 reward for information about cash smuggling; and the third makes cash smuggling a crime. One of the selling points being used to promote the bills is the fact that any cash collected from smugglers will go to the US Treasury and will reduce the amount of money it has to borrow."

KISSINGER, HAIG HOLD UNANNOUNCED MEETING WITH HELMUT SCHMIDT

Former Secretary of State **Henry Kissinger** and former NATO Commander Alexander Haig met in Monterey, California with West German Chancellor Helmut Schmidt, whose visit to the United States was not announced. Also at the meeting was Trilateralist **David Packard** and Bechtel Corp. President George Shultz. The nature of the meeting was not disclosed.

Shultz was Secretary of the Treasury and Secretary of Labor in the Nixon Administration. **Kissinger** was the Secretary of the State under Mr. Nixon, and General Haig formerly headed Mr. Nixon's White House staff and was a deputy to **Kissinger.**

Packard is a former board chairman of the Hewlett-Packard Corp. and a former Secretary of Defense.

CHASE FINDS BANKING LOOPHOLE

US banks have found a major loophole to skirt federal regulations requiring them to keep idle reserves behind deposits.

A spokesman for the Federal Reserve which oversees the reserve rules has declined opinion on whether the scheme may be a violation of federal regulations on maintaining reserves.

The official warned that banks using the loophole may be in violation of a request made by the Fed last August as part of its program to help defend the US dollar in foreign exchange transactions.

Here's how the loophole works: a US bank-holding company sells commercial paper or corporate IOU's to investors domestically. It then uses the proceeds to make deposits in a foreign branch of its subsidiary bank. That branch then relends the funds to its head office in the US.

Holding companies and foreign branches of US banks are exempt from reserve requirements.

The amounts involved are large. An analysis of the financial statements of Chase Manhattan Corp. (**David Rockefeller**), for example, indicated the company had more than $1.5 billion on deposit at midyear with foreign branches of its chief subsidiary, Chase Manhattan Bank.

US CUSTOMS AND GOLD OWNERSHIP

In the August TO we cited harrassment of Editor Antony Sutton by US Customs, en route from Vancouver, Canada to San Francisco.

A TO reader writes as follows:

"For years I have been complaining about IRS/UST [US Treasury] *re: gold. Attached is a letter that took two years to get a decent reply. The significant thing is that gold can be taken out of the US in any quantity without declaration.*

"I found Customs officers totally ignorant both in Seattle and New York on my many trips abroad."

The following quote is from a letter dated January 20, 1978 from Gene E. Godley, Assistant Secretary of Legislative Affairs, Department of the Treasury to the reader quoted above.

DEPARTMENT OF THE TREASURY,
WASHINGTON, D.C. 20220

Dear Mr. :

This is in reply to your letter dated December 26, 1977, concerning further the reporting requirements under PL 91-508, commonly known as the Bank of Secrecy Act.

You ask whether all gold coins are exempt from the reporting requirements of the Act. In that connection, Customs Circular, ENF-4-R.E.P. which has been made available to you, states on page 1 as follows:

"The Secretary of the Treasury has determined that, in addition to U.S. coin and currency, all foreign coin and currency which circulate and are customarily used and accepted as money in the issuing country must be reported when the amount being transported exceeds $5,000. Based on information currently available, gold coins do not at this time customarily circulate as money anywhere in the world; and, therefore, they do not have to be reported under 31 CFR 103."

Consequently, gold coins are not subject to the reporting requirements and a person could properly answer "No" to question 10 on the Customs Declaration, Form 6059B, which asks the traveler whether he has $5,000 or more in currency or monetary instruments, if he is transporting gold coins. However, as stated on page 2 of the Customs Circular,

> *"While not subject to the currency reporting requirements, gold coins and other coins imported for non-monetary purposes must be declared and are subject to Customs entry requirements as merchandise. Commercial shipments exported from the United States should be accompanied by the filing of a Shipper's Export Declaration."*

The Treasury wants it both ways. It does not recognize gold as money, yet wants gold declared at a port of entry because other countries recognize gold as money.

Readers should bring the "ignorance" of US Customs to the attention of interested members of Congress. If the Treasury is forced to recognize its own inconsistencies it may be another small step towards a rational monetary system.

PERSECUTION OF THE GOLD BUGS

As readers of TO well know, C.V. Myers, editor of *Myers Finance and Energy* (642 Peyton Bldg., Spokane, WA 99201) is in a Canadian jail awaiting parole.

There has been an extraordinary development in this trumped-up jailing of a foremost gold bug — the Parole Board is making release dependent upon Myers caving into the Canadian tax authorities (Revenue Canada Taxation).

Myers may well be Canada's first political prisoner.

TRILATERAL LANE KIRKLAND

Lane Kirkland has been secretary-treasurer of the AFL-CIO and second in command to George Meany since 1969.

Meany is now eighty-five and will probably retire this year.

Where Meany has realistic views about the Soviet Union and always resisted transferring US technology to the USSR (unlike big business socialists), **Lane Kirkland** reflects Trilateralist views.

Unfortunately **Kirkland** is rated "most likely" to succeed Meany.

ANOTHER TRILATERAL TASK FORCE REPORT

The Trilateral Commission has just issued another Task Force Report *Industrial Policy and the International Economy* (Triangle Paper No. 19).

At first reading the group of three authors appears to recognize the value of a market system. Indeed in the conclusions they make the following statement:

> *"A properly functioning market is the most important instrument of policy."*

However on closer reading it is more than obvious that the authors do not have the generally understood market mechanism in mind (which would of course be inconsistent with the Trilateral objective of a planned world economy).

The Task Force recommends a controlled market economy. Something of a paradox, but their proposal reads as follows:

> *". . . The report does not mean laissez faire when it supports working with market forces. Laissez faire is not the right way to get markets to work well. Enterprises cannot be trusted to remain competitive without government policing . . . markets need to be helped and complemented."*

This is, of course, nonsense. It smacks of Orwellian doublethink. A market mechanism is a free mechanism, it can only exist with laissez faire policies. The Trilaterals want to turn it upside down and invent a "controlled free enterprise," actually, planning with a "free enterprise tag."

FORMER TRILATERAL ARTHUR M. WOOD

Arthur M. Wood former chairman of Sears Roebuck, has written to Patrick M. Wood, publisher of the Trilateral Observer, to advise that he has resigned as a member of the Trilateral Commission. However, TO policy is to continue to track "former" members of the Trilateral Commission until we have evidence they have abandoned the totalitarian philosophies promoted by the organization. Similarly we regard former members of the Communist and Nazi parties with equal suspicion.

TRILATERALIST CHINA POLICY

Trilateral policy is to build Communist China with US technology and financial aid much in the same way that Wall Street built the Soviet Union in the years since 1920.

Walter Mondale, vice president, was in China for two days of significant discussions during August. Among the agreements concluded was one for "cultural exchange" and another for US assistance to Chinese hydroelectric power development. **Mondale** has asserted that the U.S. and China can "see eye to eye on a wide range of global and regional problems."

Mondale also scheduled a meeting with ten top American businessmen during his China visit and put them to considerable difficulty by insisting that the meeting take place on Chinese soil — actually, at Canton. Commented George Suter of the US Chamber of Commerce in the Philippines "Why not the face of the moon?"

Once again Trilaterals orchestrated approval which was dutifully reported in the press. For example, *The Asian Wall Street Journal* ran a lead article citing (with one minor exception) only Trilaterally connected sources or pro-Chinese trade sources. *The Asian Wall Street Journal* article cited: Kenneth P. Morse (president of Chase Pacific Trade Advisors); editor Frederic M. Kaplan of US-China People's Friendship Association; A. Doak Barnett of Brookings (the Trilateralist think tank); Stanley Young of National Council for United States-China Trade and various Chinese sources. A mild seven-line criticism was buried in the text (from Victor Li, Professor of International Law at Stanford University).

TOWARDS A WORLD ECONOMY

Trilateralism is moving the world to a New Economic World Order through merging nation-states into regional groupings.

A similar Trilateral process is taking place with corporations. They are being grouped into worldwide conglomerates under the leadership of American and European multinationals.

When the Trilateral Commission was founded, **Giovanni Agnelli** predicted this world grouping would happen quickly in the automobile industry, and a recent article in the French newspaper *Le Monde* (August 3, 1979) confirms this trend:

> *"Today nine groups control more than 80 percent of auto production worldwide, and the trend continues. General Motors, enlarging its European network, will install a new factory in Spain. Ford recently acquired 25 percent of Japan's Toyo Kogyo, maker of Mazda. Eventually Chrysler is likely to be bailed out of its troubles by a European company — perhaps Volkswagen. Honda recently signed an agreement with British Leyland for a new model to be built in Great Britain and distributed in France. Peugeot-Citroen and Volkswagen are doing well, but unless they buy out competing firms they may be unable to withstand the American offensive. Fiat is said to be preparing an important merger; and the Swedish government has recommended that Volvo and Saab collaborate with foreign manufacturers to avoid financial crisis."*

CARTER'S ADVISERS ON THE CUBAN SITUATION

Carter has sixteen advisers on the Cuban troops situation. Of these, five (plus **Carter**) are Trilaterals: **Henry Kissinger, George Ball, Sol Linowitz, David Packard and William Scranton.**

The others are all from the Eastern Establishment which has monopolized foreign policy since the turn of the century. It is notable that these Trilateralists have all been strongly in favor of aid and assistance to the Soviet Union, and it was this financial and technical subsidy which brought the Soviet Union to its present military peak.

Some had pecuniary advantage in building the USSR. For example, **David Packard** is the "Packard" in Hewlett-Packard, the giant electronics manufacturer.

PETRO CANADA

The Canadian state-owned oil giant Petro Canada has always had Trilateral representation. The current Trilateralist is Deputy Chairman **Donald Southam Harvie.**

A four man Canadian task force has recommended that most of the assets of Petro Canada be placed into a new company which will be sold to private and institutional investors in Canada. The intention is not only to make Petro Canada a private company, but a private Canadian company owned by Canadians.

The state oil concern was formed in 1975 from a takeover of Pacific Petroleums Ltd. (subsidiary of the US firm Phillips Petroleum Co.) and Atlantic Richfield Ltd. (subsidiary of Atlantic Richfield Company). Atlantic Richfield Company is, of course, closely linked to **Rockefeller** interests and its chairman, R.O. Anderson, is connected to the elitist Aspen Institute for Humanistic Studies.

On balance then, the new Canadian move represents a dual cause for celebration: Petro Canada would be returned to the private sector and away from international forces.

JAPAN

Trilateralist **Yoshizo Ikeda** is prominently mentioned to be the next Japanese Ambassador to the United States.

In order to work a Trilateral into this important post the Japanese government has had to break a long tradition that such officers come from within the Japanese foreign ministry.

Yoshizo Ikeda is chairman of Mitsui & Co. and is, of course, a businessman with no knowledge of Japanese foreign affairs.

The Japanese Minister of External Economic Affairs, **Nobuhiko Ushiba,** is already a Trilateralist, so this would give Trilateralists almost a monopoly on Japanese representation in the United States.

IRAN

It is reported reliably that the Shah of Iran has placed a "substantial" amount of his personal fortune, estimated at $17 billion, with the Chase Manhattan Bank. The Shah's account is "personally handled by Chase Chairman **David Rockefeller.**" (*Mid-East Report,* October 1, 1979)

Recently both **David Rockefeller** and **Henry Kissinger,** who is on the Chase International Advisory Committee, visited the Shah at his residence in Cuernavaca, Mexico. One wonders how **Henry Kissinger** knows enough about financial matters to advise the Shah?

THE TRILATERAL ATTACK ON THE MEDIA

As we mentioned earlier in this issue, the Trilateral attack on the media can be used to our advantage — to alert the media and gain the media as an ally.

In *The Crisis of Democracy* by Michel J. Crozier (a Trilateral Commission report published in 1975 by New York University Press, whose president is also a Trilateral, **John C. Sawhill**), we read (page 182): ". . . There is also the need to assure the government the right and the ability to withhold information at the source."

And on page 181 we read on "freedom of the press":

". . . It is a freedom which can be abused . . . The responsibility of the press should now be increased to be commensurate with its power: significant measures are required to restore an appropriate balance between the press, the government and other institution in society."

The Trilateral report then goes on to propose a government regulatory agency to protect "the broader interests of society and government."

This censorship cry has now been picked up by non-Trilaterals, who presumably know where the power lies. For example:

James Schlesinger — "I know that a free society cannot survive without a free press. Right now we are testing whether a free society can survive with a free press."

House Democratic Leader Jim Wright — "Washington reporters have become the enemies of government . . . I think we all ought to be on the same team, the same side."

Remember: there can be no modification of the First Amendment without taking the first step to a totalitarian society.

RICHARD M. NIXON

In case you didn't catch it in your local newpaper, Richard M. Nixon has purchased a $750,000 New York townhouse at 142 East 65th Street — next door to a double townhouse occupied by **David Rockefeller**, chairman of Chase Manhattan.

WASHINGTON, D.C.

The Mayor of Washington, D.C., Marion Barry, is pushing the idea that Washington, D.C. become an international city with its own Office of Protocol. This is essential for Trilateral New Economic World Order objectives and needs to be watched.

WALL STREET JOURNAL

A couple of months back a TO reader had an exchange of letters with Frederick Taylor, editor of the *Wall Street Journal*.

Taylor evidently believes that "one world" economy is not a Trilateral objective because one of his Trilateral friends told him so. Perhaps a couple of TO readers will now take the time to send Taylor a copy of the booklet just issued by TO reproducing the Council Bluffs radio interview with **George Franklin, Jr.,** coordinator of the Trilateral Commission.

To be sure, **Franklin** denies "one world" as an objective — and we were able to cite specific paragraphs from Trilateral publications to show Franklin lied.

1980

ANOTHER TRILATERALIST COVER UP

The following attempted cover-up recently took place on Radio Station WROC (Rochester, New York). The commentator was Tony Gold interviewing Trilateral **John B. Anderson.**

A question was called in by Mrs. Ruth Colby, president of the Monroe County Chapter of the Committee to Restore the Constitution:

Colby: "I have in front of me Triangle Paper #12 and you are listed as one of the members of this particular task force concerning the Problem of International Consultations. OK, are you there?"

Anderson: *"Yes, Ma'am."*

Colby: "OK, now I am very concerned about one particular part of this report and I wondered if you wanted to comment on it. It's on page 17 and what it says is this: 'If a more effective and equitable economic order is to emerge, national policies and programs must be subject to moderation and adjustment to take into account probable adverse international ramifications. This can be accomplished only if powerful domestic agencies are brought under control and sensitized to the international consequences of their policies.'

"*Now this Trilateral process is going on outside the government of the United States in a private organization. It's my understanding that this kind of thing is quite illegal. I wonder if you'd like to comment on it.*"

Anderson: "*Ma'am, I don't know exactly what paper it is that you refer to or under whose imprimatur that paper was published but I'm not proposing, I can assure you, that any laws and regulations be adopted by any private organization that would have the place of supplanting or taking the place of a legislative body in this country. I'm not sponsoring a proposal of that kind. I don't know whose proposal you are reading from, but its certainly not my idea and I wouldn't subscribe to that doctrine.*"

EDITORIAL COMMENT:

(1) I have checked Mrs. Colby's extract from *Triangle Paper #12*. It is precisely as she called it in over the air. Readers may see it for themselves on Paper #12 (page 17) obtainable from the Trilateral Commission, 345 East 46th Street, New York, NY 10017.

(2) **John B. Anderson's** name appears on page IV of the same Paper #12 as a person consulted by the writers in preparing the report.

FRENCH TRILATERAL VIOLATES THE CONSTITUTION OF FRANCE

We have noted that American Trilaterals care little for the Constitution of the United States — at least that is the clear impression from their writings.

It now appears that **Raymond Barre,** Prime Minister of

France and a Trilateral cares little for the Constitution of France.

The Constitutional Council, a kind of referee between the executive and legislative branches of the French government, normally a quiescent sort of organization, has found **Barre** in violation of the Constitution — an unprecedented finding.

Barre attempted to bulldoze his budget without a vote of the National Assembly on the expenditure section.

BANK DEADBEATS

Trilateral bankers figure prominently among major banks refusing to pay debts owed the US Treasury. About $8 million is owed by banks who have erroneously cashed checks with forged endorsements.

The excuse put forward by Chase Manhattan is,

"This is money frequently owed to us by other banks. . ."

Says Bank Of America, which owes the largest amount, *"There's been no pressure from Treasury . . ."* (*Washington Post,* December 2, 1979)

The money has been owed since 1970. Imagine what would happen to a poor taxpayer who owed the Treasury a few hundred or thousand dollars and refused to pay up! Obviously, its one rule for the big banks, heavily represented in Trilateralism, and another rule for the "peons."

CHASE MANHATTAN BANK

Top management at Chase is being shuffled. **David Rockefeller** remains as chairman of the board until 1981 but will hand over the powers of chief executive officer to Willard Carlisle Butcher. Butcher is a prominent lecturer on the "free enterprise system" and reportedly a master at compromise solutions.

LETTERS FROM READERS

Letters from readers on our "what can be done" issue, generally support our position that information comes first followed by a one-on-one approach to fellow citizens.

One or two readers suggest this be supported by a "refusal to cooperate." In other words "ignore the state" so long as it refuses to abide by the Constitution.

When we look at what is happening to the Fourth Amendment (the Internal Revenue Service has been supported by the courts in its trampling on the Fourth Amendment, i.e., right to due process of law) and the First Amendment (ask any member of the press whether freedom of speech is in danger — and these readers may find some sympathetic support).

RHODESIA

Lord Carrington, the British Foreign Secretary who put together the Rhodesia settlement is a Trilateral.

The previous British Foreign Secretary was **David Owen** — he was pushing openly for a Patriotic Front dictatorship.

MILITARY AID TO THE SOVIET UNION

The **Carter** administration is continuing the Nixon-Ford administration policy of military aid to the Soviet Union — with retribution against any American who exposes the covert cooperation.

Jack Anderson recently surfaced the case of Larry Brady, a Commerce Department analyst who protested that the trucks used by the Soviets to invade Afghanistan were American engineered and that the agreement with the Soviets deliberately left out the standard promise that the technology would not be used for military purposes. **Kissinger** is the key figure in this episode.

Larry Brady is being persecuted by Commerce and the administration for protesting this cooperation.

A similar episode happened to this editor back in 1972 at the Hoover Institution. When protesting the military potential in the Kama Truck Plant and the export of ball bearing machining equipment (for Soviet missiles), this editor came under strong pressure to keep quiet.

David Packard is a prominent trustee of the Hoover Institution.

NO END TO IT. . .

Trilateral **A.M. Solomon,** Under Secretary for Monetary Affairs at the Treasury, has been appointed president of the New York Federal Reserve Bank replacing Trilateral **Paul Volcker,** who left last year to become chairman of the Federal Reserve Board in Washington D.C., replacing Trilateral **Arthur F. Burns** in that position.

Comments on **Solomon's** appointment in the *Wall Street Journal* (Trilateral **J. Paul Austin** is a director of parent company, Dow Jones) were, naturally, from Trilateralists:

- *"..an ideal choice."* — **Robert V. Roosa**
- *"I delighted to have Tony Solomon join the Federal Reserve System. . ."* — **Paul Volcker**
- *"I know of few individuals who have had as broad an exposure to and experience in dealing first hand with the challenges of international economic affairs."* — Willard C. Butcher (president and CEO of Chase Manhattan Bank)

We note that **Anthony Solomon** was the bank's "first choice," that the decision was made last November, but **Solomon** needed "time to consider." Presumably the triumph of gold over Trilateral fiat monetary schemes was the final straw prompting **Solomon's** move.

THE WALL STREET JOURNAL

Wall Street Journal editors refuse to recognize the Trilateral Commission. The above reported item on the appointment of **Anthony Solomon** occupied twenty-seven column inches in the January 22nd issue on the key page two. With the exception of one inch devoted to the comment of Jerry L. Jordan of Pittsburgh National Bank, the rest of the article (twenty-six inches) was devoted to comments by a group of "revolving door" Trilaterals. This was not mentioned by *WSJ.*

We have a choice of assuming either:

- (a) *Wall Street Journal* is so naive it can't see a story even when it prints one, or
- (b) The news filter that screens out the TC is firmly in place (**J. Paul Austin** is a director of Dow Jones.)

(c) *WSJ* editors have decided that saying nothing is better than invoking the "wrath" of this super-powerful elite.

Interested readers should remind *Wall Street Journal* editors of a principle of scientific methodology: The most general explanation of a phenomenon is the most acceptable explanation. The general explanation of the above article is Trilateralism; it repeats throughout the article. Why wasn't this recognized by *WSJ* writers?

TRILATERALS BACKING DOWN ON GOLD?

As we have noted in several issues, Trilaterals have a vehement dislike for gold. A planned world economy requires a fiat monetary system and gold grants individual sovereignty.

Among these Trilaterals, **Robert Roosa** (partner in Brown Brothers, Harriman) has been among the strongest and most active opponents of gold. He is now singing a slightly different tune. A recent interview provided the following quotation:

"In this terribly uncertain world gold always has some sort of grip on the minds of men . . . it lends a little mythical support to central banks and their creation of paper money and it remains a good war chest in the event everything breaks down . . . "

Roosa, more than any other single man, is responsible for the unworkable patchwork mess of agreements and practices that today pass for an international monetary system. Without being held accountable for his financial blunders of the last 15 years, the press is allowing him to talk his way into a position of reasonable sensibility.

ROCKEFELLER FUNDING OF GEORGE BUSH

Several readers have enquired about the source of our statement that **David Rockefeller** was the source of $5,000 funding for fellow Trilateralist **George Bush.**

"When Bush decided, or was directed, to run for the Presidency, it was **David Rockefeller** who immediately gave him $5,000, the maximum possible contribution at the time, for the **'Bush** For President Committee,' and has given him much more since that time." — Don Bell Reports, P.O. Box 2223, Palm Beach, Florida 33480 - $24.00 per year.

TOWARDS A FASCIST AMERICA

Jimmy Carter is reviving the President's Executive Exchange Program created originally in 1970 under Richard Nixon. Robert E. Kirby, chairman of Westinghouse Electric Corporation, has been named chairman of a commission to oversee the project. As *Business Week* phrases the intention:

"The aim has been to make the bureaucrats more knowledgeable about the business they might be regulating and the corporate executives more sophisticated about the political and social constraints involved in government decisions."

Business Week might have added that this close interlock beween state and business is a hallmark of the fascist economy.

TRILATERALS AND THEIR IRAN CRISIS

We have pointed out before that Trilateralists achieve their goal of a socialist planned world economy by "crisis management." Iran is a case study in "crisis management." This time, once again, US national interests were sacrificed and American lives placed in jeopardy by special interests using their political power for personal ends. The following key facts are known and can be supported at this time:

- The Shah was brought to the United States by **Henry Kissinger** and **David Rockefeller**. As Mary McCrory wrote in *The Washington Star* (November 27, 1979): "Kissinger. . .is the principal architect of the current catastrophe in Iran. Working with **David Rockefeller** he persuaded a reluctant administration to admit the Shah to the United States out of compassion."

- Numerous warnings from Iran were made to the State Department and widely known in the administration that the embassy would be in danger if the Shah was admitted. These date back to February, 1979, when armed Iranians held 100 US Embassy personnel hostage for nearly two hours.

- Defenses at the embassy were not beefed up after this February attack by orders of the "seventh floor at the State Department." (This is the office of Trilaterals **Cyrus Vance** and **Warren Christopher.**) State security personnel were prevented from implementing security.
- **Rockefeller** and **Kissinger** called in elitist, establishment attorney, John J. McCloy to apply pressure to obtain visas for the Shah and his group. The Shah had no need of urgent medical treatment. This was a cover story.
- The Shah was induced to invest his funds (estimates range from $1/2 billion to $25 billion) with Chase Manhattan. **David Rockefeller** is chairman of Chase Manhattan and **Kissinger** is chairman of the Chase International Advisory Committee.

We can rightfully conclude the Shah was used (and he says as much in his memoirs) by major financial interests for their own purposes.

RONALD REAGAN

We do not altogether like the make-up of the Reagan campaign organization. A close advisor is **Caspar W. Weinberger,** Trilateralist and vice-president of the Bechtel Corporation. Also, William Casey, Reagan's finance committee chairman was the former Securities and Exchange Commission chairman. . . and has past connections with Armand Hammer.

ALDEN W. CLAUSEN

The president of Bank of America, **Clausen** is a former Trilateralist. Although we have no record that **Clausen** ever renounced his membership in the Commission and its ideals, a recent speech he gave seemed out of line with the usual Trilateral Commission rhetoric. In the speech **Clausen** blasted the **Carter** administration and its policies: "The Administration [sic] is only too willing to point to rising world oil prices, international tensions and other developments ostensibly beyond their control as the primary causes of our problems. That is simply not true. Most of our difficulties are right here at home. Government is spending beyond its means. . . our economy is spinning its wheels in regulatory mud. . . " **Clausen** went on to say that we spend more on regulatory controls than on investment in new productive equipment.

We are willing to accept **Clausen's** speech at face value and hope that he will soon turn his attention to other Trilateral policies.

THE CRUISE MISSILE

General Dynamics Convair in San Diego has worked on cruise missiles since 1972 and expected to receive the recent Air Force contract ($1 - 2 billion in value) for the construction of the air-launched missile. Instead, the massive contract went to Boeing. There are now claims heard of "politics" in the awarding of the contract. While most San Diegans are looking to the political pressure wielded by Senators Jackson and Magnuson as the *Realpolitik* behind the Boeing Contract, TO thinks otherwise. We would suggest that the San Diegans look to **T.A. Wilson,** chairman of the board of Boeing Company, and Boeing director, **Harold Brown,** US Secretary of Defense, both of whom are members of the Trilateral Commission. Once again the Trilateral Commission has been a device used to accumulate benefits and immense profits for its members.

DID KISSINGER, FORD ET AL TAKE BRIBES?

Early on the morning of March 6 the Associated Press wire carried an extraordinary story that the Shah had questionable business dealings with several prominent Americans, including some we know to be Trilateral Commissioners. According to the story, documents to this effect in the possession of the Central Bank of Iran were given to the UN Investigating Commission which visited Iran.

This story appeared in a few newspapers around the US, and was summararily dropped. We have seen no reports since March 6. Briefly, the story that came over the AP wires was that **David Rockefeller** had a "shady" carpet deal and gifts from the Shah; that **Henry Kissinger** had received "bribes"; that Gerald Ford had received money and so on. AP could not reach **Kissinger** and **Rockefeller** for comment, and Ford told AP that it was a "categorical lie." We would appreciate any further information on this that readers could obtain, especially a copy of the index or the documents issued by the Central Bank of Iran. There is not enough information available to pass judgement, *but* we want to know why the story apparently was killed. Normally such accusations are investigated.

TRADE UNIONS AND TRILATERALISM

There is an increasing gap between rank and file trade unionists and the top-echelon unionists — the union bosses — who have in many cases allied themselves with the Trilateralists.

A recent example we are aware of is the split in the United Auto Workers. The president of *United Auto Workers Local #1250,* Thomas R. Payne, criticised the UAW International president, Douglas A. Fraser, with keeping silent about "loss of jobs and secret plans that Ford or any other company might have with foreign governments." **Philip Caldwell,** president of Ford Motor Company, recently joined the Trilateral Commission. The interests of individual trade unionists differ greatly from those of top leadership that are working with the globalists.

LANE KIRKLAND

Commissioner **Lane Kirkland** is proving to be much more amenable to the multinationals than George Meany. Recently he spent a weekend with the heavyweights of American industry (including many Trilaterals) at the Business Council in Virginia.

PHILIP CALDWELL

Commissioner **Philip Caldwell,** chairman of Ford Motor Company, appears not to have heard of the Trilateral process. According to Trilateralism, Japan, Europe and North America are working together jointly in an interdependent world. Yet **Caldwell** recently called on the US Government to keep Japanese autos out of the US market. Said **Caldwell:** "We have a market, why don't we get something out of it?"

The crux of the matter is that sloppy management, and too much interest in world politics, had led Ford and other

American auto companies into a trap: even rank and file employees on the assembly line knew what top management did not — Americans wanted smaller, fuel-efficient automobiles.

THE CENSUS

Hardly anyone believed claims that the 1980 Census was confidential, and now those beliefs are supported. The *San Francisco Examiner* has published details from the census return filed by Mayor Diane Feinstein, even down to the fact that Feinstein used a ball point pen instead of the required pencil.

J. PAUL AUSTIN

Austin, part of the inner clique behind **Jimmy Carter,** is in trouble at Coca-Cola, where he is presently chairman of the board.

The former chairman of the board and "granddaddy" of Coca-Cola is Robert W. Woodruff. Now 90 years old, Woodruff retired from Coke some 25 years ago, after running the giant company since 1923. He reportedly views debt with some disdain, and is not too happy with recent Coke profit figures or its ventures into the debt markets, all of which is **Austin** inspired.

There is evidence that Woodruff and other members of the board are reducing **Austin's** powers. The new president is Roberto C. Goizueta, who is relatively unknown and almost certainly not an **Austin** choice. Other reports suggest **Austin** is looking for a top-level political post.

CYRUS VANCE

Former Secretary of State **Cyrus Vance** has joined the board of IBM.

Vance is a partner in the establishment law firm of Simpson, Thacher & Bartlett and was previously an IBM director from 1969 to 1976.

Simpson, Thacher & Bartlett is of historical interest because of its assistance to the Bolshevik Revolution in 1917.

WALL STREET JOURNAL AGAIN

The *Wall Street Journal* has apparently been stung by criticism of its blind eye where Trilaterals are concerned. Here are extracts from a May 1, 1980 editorial. Not much, but a start:

"There is no question that the Trilateral Commission elitist group, with all the advantages and liabilities that elitism entails . . .

"President Carter is a former Trilateralist, as are 17 past or present members of his government, plus the chairman of the Republican National Committee and the president of the AFL-CIO.

"The commission members brought into government by Carter include both Zbigniew Brzezinski, his hawkish national-security adviser, and outgoing Secretary of State Cyrus R. Vance, with whom Brzezinski has had a running policy battle for more than three years.

"The list also includes both Defense Secretary Harold Brown, who supports the MX missile and the buildup of a rapid-deployment force, and superdove Paul Warnke, the former arms-control director.

"The Trilateral Commission is fair game, or should be, for criticism that it is an excessively elitist group that it issues unnecessarily dull reports that are, in fact, not very widely read. But a 'Communist-accommodating' conspiracy?

"Come on, now."

MUSICAL CHAIRS

We have previously reported on the interlocks between the two leading Trilateral banks: Chase Manhattan of New York and First Chicago Corp. The ties are even closer after a recent shuffling of top positions.

On April 28, 1980 the board of First Chicago fired chairman and chief executive officer A. Robert Abboud (not a Trilateral). On Tuesday, June 24, it named Barry F. Sullivan (executive vice president of Chase Manhattan) to become the new chairman and chief executive officer. The following day Thomas G. Labrecque of Chase Manhattan was named president of Chase

Manhattan to replace Willard C. Butcher who will replace
David Rockefeller next year as chairman of Chase Manhattan.
David Rockefeller is moving into the background?

ELECTION UPDATE: RONALD REAGAN

Common Cause — the self-styled citizens lobby founded by
Rockefeller and his elitist friends — has gone into court to
challenge the independent committees founded to support
Reagan. Common Cause has asked the court to declare such
expenditures to be illegal.

Common Cause was run by **John Gardner** (CFR) and was
financed originally by:

David Packard
Caspar Weinberger
John D. Rockefeller II
Howard Stein (Dreyfus Fund)
Andrew Heiskell (Time, Inc.)
Thomas Watson (IBM and CFR)
John Hay (CFR)
Sol Linowitz (CFR and Trilateral)

RONALD REAGAN'S BUSINESS ADVISORY PANEL

The following is a list of the 40 members of Ronald Reagan's
Business Advisory Panel:

William N. Agee, chairman and CEO, General
Telephone & Electronics Corp. of Stamford, Conn.

Herbert M. Dwight, Jr., president and chairman,
Spectra Physics Inc. of Mountain View, Calif.

Noel Fenton, president, Acurex Corp. of Mountain
View, Calif.

Kipling Hagopian, partner, Brentwood Associates of
Los Angeles.

Ned Heizer, chairman and president, Heizer Corp. of
Chicago.

Charles Lea, managing director, New Court Securities
of New York.

J. Paul Lyet, chairman and chief executive officer,
Sperry Corp. of New York.

M. Kenneth Oshman, president and chief executive officer, Rolm Corp. of Santa Clara, Calif.

W.J. Sanders III, chairman, president and CEO, Advanced Micro Devices, Inc., of Sunnyvale, Calif.

Sidney Topol, chairman and president, Scientific-Atlanta Inc. of Atlanta.

Edwin V.P. Zschau, chairman, System Industries of Sunnyvale, Calif.

Charles Schwab, president of Charles Schwab Corp.

Ray C. Adam, chairman and CEO, N. L. Industries, Inc.

Robert H.B. Baldwin, president, Morgan Stanley & Co. Inc.

William M. Batten, chairman and CEO, New York Stock Exchange.

Robert A. Beck, chairman and CEO, Prudential Life Insurance Co.

Alfred Brittian III, chairman and CEO, Bankers Trust Corp.

Fletcher L. Byrom, chairman and CEO, Koppers Co., Inc. of Pittsburgh

J.R. Fluor, chairman and CEO, Fluor Corp.

John W. Hanley, chairman and CEO, Monsanto Co.

Edward G. Harness, chairman and CEO, Proctor & Gamble Co.

Robert S. Hatfield, chairman and CEO, The Continental Group Inc.

Philip M. Hawley, president and CEO, Carter Hawley Hale Stores Inc.

William A. Hewitt, chairman and CEO, Deere & Co.

Paul Howell, chairman and president, Howell Corp.

Robert L. James, chairman and CEO, The Marschalk Co.

Leonard A. Lauder, president, Estee-Lauder Corp.

Thomas A. Maciooe, president and CEO, Allied Stores Corp.

Shaw Mudge, Sr., president and CEO, Shaw Mudge Co.

Charles J. Pilliod Jr., chairman and CEO, Goodyear Tire & Rubber Co.

Edmund T. Pratt. Jr., chairman and CEO, Pfizer Inc.

Malcolm M. Prine, president and chairman, Ryan Homes, Inc.

Donald T. Regan, chairman, Merrill Lynch & Co., Inc.

Toby Schreiber, president and chairman, Bethlehem Steel Corp.

Richard P. Schubert, vice chairman, Bethlehem Steel Corp.

Richard R. Shinn, chairman and CEO, Metropolitan Life Insurance Co.

Frederick W. Smith, chairman and CEO, General Express Corp.

George H. Weyerhaeuser, president and CEO, Weyerhaeuser Co.

John C. Whitehead, co-chairman, Goldman, Sachs & Co.

We have already reported the following Trilaterals as close to Reagan:

David Packard

Caspar Weinberger

Anne Armstrong

We can now add from the above list:

Philip M. Hawley

William A. Hewitt

George H. Weyerhaeuser

At least a half dozen other names on this list are men with close associations with Trilaterals. For example, *William N. Agee* (Bendix), *Charles Lea* (New Court Securities), *Robert S. Hatfield* (Continental Corporation).

ANDERSON AND THE MEDIA

Some Trilateral influence of CBS and NBC surfaced at the Republican National Convention.

CBS News used Bill Moyers and James Kilpatrick for network coverage. Moyers is closely connected with the Aspen Institute (covered in September, 1980 issue of TO). Kilpatrick is a "conservative" who manages to keep close to the establishment party line on most issues.

NBC News continued its policy of using news makers as news analysts. Previously, NBC hired **Henry Kissinger** for $1 million as a commentator on foreign policy. Then Gerald Ford was hired to comment on the White House. At the Republican National Convention, "independent" candidate **John Anderson** was hired to comment on the primaries.

Lyn Nofziger (Reagan's media advisor) commented, "I think it's a campaign contribution from NBC to **John Anderson.** Certainly, at least, the hiring of **Anderson** is a violation of the "equal time" provision of Section 315 of the Communications Act.

B. DALTON BOOKSELLER BLACKLISTS T.O.W.

Trilaterals Over Washington is a "best seller," i.e., over 40,000 copies. With extensive radio and TV appearances recently made by coauthors Sutton and Wood, it was no surprise that a B. Dalton Booksellers' (one of the country's largest book store chains) representative called to inquire about stocking their 550 retail outlets with T.O.W. They had apparently had many requests from all over the country, and word had filtered to the home office.

After sending Dalton a "review copy" of T.O.W., there was no further word from Dalton regarding a purchase order. After several days had passed, a call placed to Dalton headquarters was met with "We're sorry, but we're not interested in carrying your book."

How can a major bookstore chain turn away a *best seller* that has demand throughout their system?

This is suppression and blacklisting at its worst.

ROCKEFELLER SHAREHOLDINGS IN OIL INDUSTRY

The Corporate Data Exchange (CDE), a non-profit research organization based in New York, has issued a report on

Rockefeller holdings in major oil companies.

EXXON: Largest of all oil companies and has the largest annual gross income of any US based corporation. The Rockefeller family holds 7.7 million shares, or 1.7% of outstanding stock. Chase Manhattan holds another 1.8%.

MARATHON: The family holds 305,000, or 1% of the stock.

MOBIL: Rockefellers hold 1.9 million shares, or 1.8%, and Chase owns another 1.4%.

STANDARD OIL OF CALIFORNIA: They hold 3.6 million shares (2.1%) and Chase holds 1.4%.

STANDARD OIL OF INDIANA: The Rockefellers own 1.2 million shares, 0.8%, while Chase has 1.2%.

These figures apparently do not include minority holdings in other energy companies *or* proxies held and voted through trust department holdings for others. Both categories are substantial.

PERSONNEL SWITCHES

First National Bank of Chicago has been noted as one of the prime backers of Trilateralism. In a recent management reshuffle, the chairman and CEO, A. Robert Abboud, lost his job to a Chase Manhattan executive.

Now Abboud has been named president and CEO of Occidental Petroleum of Los Angeles.

The founder and present chairman of Occidental is Armand Hammer, who is well known to TO readers for his intimate involvement with the Soviet Union since 1919. Julius Hammer, Armand's father, was secretary of the Communist Party U.S.A. in 1919.

Incidental note: Former Senator Albert Gore is executive vice-president and a director of Occidental. His son, Congressman Albert A. Gore, Jr., of Tennessee serves on the Oversight Subcommittee of the House Commerce Committee.

HEDLEY DONOVAN

In August 1979 **Donovan** filled a newly created position titled, "Senior Advisor to the President." As former editor-in-chief of TIME, Inc., he brought his wide range of expertise to President **Carter's** assistance.

By our estimation, **Donovan's** primary work in the White House was to organize the President's Commission for a National Agenda for the 1980's. This group will issue its report later this year.

USSR: BIOLOGICAL WARFARE

In April 1980, sufficient Anthrax germs were released in Sverdlovsk, Russia, to kill between 40 and 1,000 people.

Production of anthrax is a direct violation of the 1975 Biological Warfare Convention. Senator William Proxmire wants the **Carter** administration to take the violation to the United Nations.

We note that under Trilateral policies enunciated in *Collaboration With Communist Countries in Managing Global Problems* (*Triangle Paper #13*), emphasis is placed on "cooperative management of US-Soviet problems."

Accordingly, Trilateral **Warren Christopher** (Deputy Secretary of State), under instructions from President **Carter,** has met with Senator Proxmire to explain that the issue should not be treated in a way which would "embarrass the Soviets."

We urge Senator Proxmire to push his case. Anthrax is a deadly disease. If the Soviets are producing even small quantities of anthrax, it poses a tremendous threat to their *own people*, and to the US as well. The Soviets have already shown their propensity to use chemical warfare in Afghanistan.

CHASE MANHATTAN PREMIUM

Chase is offering customers who open a new personal savings account, a "Free Banker Bear from Chase" — a cuddly little teddy bear. This is supposedly a "good will" gesture.

Given the close Rockefeller-Chase relationship with the Russian Bear since the Bolshevik Revolution in 1917, this is a very unfortunate and inappropriate choice of give-a-way premium for Chase.

UMBERTO AGNELLI

A prominent Trilateralist and a member of the T.C.

European Executive Committee, **Agnelli** has resigned as managing director of Fiat, S.p.A. It is paradoxical that **Agnelli** is strongly opposed to a current plan to allow Nissan Motor Company of Japan into the Italian automobile market in a joint venture with state-owned automaker Alfa Romeo.

KISSINGER: REPUBLICAN CONVENTION

Henry Kissinger's involvement in the negotiations between Ronald Reagan and Gerald Ford on the co-Presidency proposal reminds us of a paragraph in **Brzezinski's** book, *Between Two Ages,* concerning the need to change the Constitution. While **Kissinger's** proposal was so outrageous and unconstitutional that it was thrown out of the convention, it shows his Trilateral audacity and forthrightness of purpose: to change the basic structure of the United States.

GALLUP-KETTERING POLL

Readers will note from the global education article that George Gallup is a trustee of the Kettering Foundation, which is an important backer of the Trilateral Commission *and* globalism.

A joint project of Gallup Poll and the Charles F. Kettering Foundation examining public attitudes to education has just been published. They wanted to find out potential resistance in the citizenry at large, but the results can hardly please the globalists:

- Only 6 percent of respondents gave the schools an "A" rating (compared to 6 percent last year and 18 percent in 1974).
- The public favors local school boards "to have greatest influence" by 68 percent."
  However, one statistic they can use, albeit out of context, is:
- 79 percent favored "morals and moral behavior instruction."

But how many of those questioned understood that the questions referred to "values education" *a la Gallup, Kettering et al.*

MACHINE READABLE PASSPORTS

The United Nations International Civil Aviation Organization (UNICAO) is promoting the use of a machine readable passport. Passport holders will be coded and numbered so that passports can be read optically at all check points.

Inconsistent with globalist arguments of removing all international barriers? Well, logic musn't interfere with practicality!

TRILATERALS AND ENERGY

Trilateral **John Sawhill** is **Carter's** choice to be chairman of the US Synthetic Fuels Corporation — an *$88 billion* boondoggle to "aid" the energy companies.

WHO IS POPULAR?

The *Wall Street Journal* and Gallup Poll conducted a joint survey among chief executives: "Who is the most respected business executive?"

David Rockefeller placed a beleagured *16th* on the list. Robert O. Anderson of the Aspen Institute fared even worse in *19th place*. In fact, out of the top twenty cited as "respected", only three are Trilaterals (**Clausen, Rockefeller** and **Shepherd**).

This poll makes nonsense of the Trilateral argument that Commissioners are chosen for administrative position because they have the respect of their peers and are "the best" for the job.

The poll supports the TO argument that Trilaterals are more likely chosen because they are compatible with **Rockefeller's** view of the world.

RHODESIA BETRAYED BY TRILATERAL

Ian Smith has made it official. Rhodesia was betrayed by Trilateral **Lord Carrington,** who was in charge of British negotiations over Rhodesia. Smith recently stated:

> *"The fatal mistake was in allowing the guerillas to retain their arms in the assembly points. One of the last assurances given at Lancaster House* [meeting place in London] *was that they would not. We were taken for a ride."*

When the world "establishment" could not get rid of Rhodesia by any other means (economic embargo, terrorists and guerillas, etc.), the only resort was to lie to the Rhodesian leadership and trick them into going along with the transition to Marxist rule.

SUTTON ON NATIONWIDE TV BROADCAST

On September 16, 1980 at 10:00 P.M. EST, Cable News Network in Atlanta aired a live one-hour nationwide broadcast on the Trilateral Commission. Interviewed were Antony Sutton, Lawrence Shoup and Trilateral **Phillip Trezise.** Shoup is a self-acclaimed Marxist and authored *The Carter Presidency: 1980 and Beyond*, which is critical of Trilaterals. **Trezise** is a former Secretary of State for Economic Affairs and is current with the Brookings Institution.

Shoup's outspoken manner did little but necessitate a reprimand from the interviewer during an early commercial break.

Trezise first tried to sell the "naive" aspect of the Commission, then broke to insults, evasion and at several points, denied demonstrable facts. When questioned about the Commission task force report *Crisis in Democracy,* **Trezise** flatly denied that the Commission published it. The interviewer had done her homework and jumped on the opportunity to correct **Trezise** on the facts. **Trezise** further denied that the Commission has "New Economic World Order" objectives, although there are dozens of places in Commission literature that this objective is clearly stated or alluded to.

While CNN was eminently fair in setting up the show to bring all sides to light, the program ended on a sour note when **Trezise** attacked CNN by calling the show "an exercise in demonology."

One gets the impression that Trilaterals are prickly about criticism.

TALKING TO TRILATERALS

Many of you have the opportunity once in a while to engage in debate with Trilateral or Council on Foreign Relations members, Humanists, legislators, etc. Some advice that will work for you:

- Calm understatement is always more effective than heated overstatement.
- Always be polite and restrained. While your typical opponent will tend to be autocratic, don't be tempted to argue.
- Stay with the facts. *Admit* you don't know something when you don't know. Have *documentation* of what you *do know* at your fingertips, and don't let them evade the subject.
- Prepare just a few topics of discussion. You can't blame *everything* on the Commission or any other group. Be realistic and fair.

CONFLICT IN ENERGY REPORTS

The government and the media have been telling us that there are grave shortages of oil. Now that Iran and Iraq are in the midst of military conflict, Deputy Energy Secretary **John Sawhill** is telling us that world oil stocks are high and global production is 2.4 million barrels a day above demand. To quote Mr. **Sawhill**: "an Iraq-Iran cutoff would be less damaging than in the past."

Sawhill predicts an increase in prices for oil due to the current problem but has no idea what the increase will be.

RUSSIAN TRADE EMBARGO

When President **Carter** announced the trade embargo against the Soviet Union after the Afghanistan invasion, his intention was for all US allies to participate. However, it seems that France and West Germany felt that the embargo didn't apply to in their case. They took the opportunity to increase trade with the Soviets rather than diminish it.

What has occured through the actions of the French and the West Germans is that Japan has suffered economic loss. The Japanese Foreign Minister Masayoshi Ito said his government adhered to the embargo strictly, while firms from France and West Germany had filled the gap. Ito is concerned that the trade between Western Europe and the USSR will "mushroom."

It appears that greed knows no boundries — political, philosophical or otherwise.

US - CHINA TRADE

The US and China are discussing agreements that would increase shipping and commercial air services between the two countries. The US delegation is led by US Treasury Secretary G. William Miller, former head of the Federal Reserve and a member of the Chase International Advisory Committee.

Miller said the Chinese will explain their new economic initiatives which, according to **C. Fred Bergsten** would benefit the US by opening China to greater international trade. **Bergsten** reported, "The importance is obvious considering that we just cut off a lot of trade with the Soviets following their invasion of Afghanistan."

It would seem this is the reason that the US delegation agreed to sell the Chinese a highly sophisticated computer that can be used to help explore for oil as well as for military purposes. It also would account for the 400 export licenses to be used for that sale of sophisticated electronic gear.

We note that it is reported in the August issue of *Reader's Digest* that IBM 360 and 370 computers are the mainstay in the Warsaw Pact Defense System. It is ironic that the US is supplying technology and weapons to both sides of a conflict that will someday surely result in the bloodiest war in history.

Again, we see that economic greed knows no bounds.

TRILATERALS & REAGAN

The Trilateral Commission admits that many of its US members are influential enough to be able to pick up a phone and reach the President direct or at least get an appointment to see him. This is reasonable in that **Carter** is a former member of the Commission - but what about Ronald Reagan if he is elected?

It was reported on September 11 that the coordinator of the Commission, **George Franklin,** stated: "**David Rockefeller** is a fairly staunch Republican and always has been. In 1976 he supported [Gerald] Ford and this time he is supporting

[Ronald] Reagan."

Some will say this is just **Franklin's** opinion. However, on September 6 the Reagans gave a dinner party at their leased country home near Washington, D.C. Attendants included **William Brock, Henry Kissinger** and **David Rockefeller.**

However attractive and well intentioned Reagan might be, one must face the fact that he is *surrounded and supported by Trilaterals.* What kind of policies can we expect if he is elected President? Nationalism and globalism mix like oil and water — they are by definition mutually exclusive.

THE FOURTH WORLD ALLIANCE

A news item of major future significance was almost totally ignored by the US press.

The shunned nations of the world -- South Africa, Taiwan and Israel have formed an alliance. All three nations are under pressure from the Communist world and the Anglo-American elite. The Third World likewise does not view these nations with particular favor.

Although small and geographically distant from each other, South Africa, Taiwan and Israel are not under-developed. They are technologically capable and have the expertise to manufacture advanced weaponry, including atomic weapons. South Africa has uranium and an advanced process to extract plutonium that is less costly and more efficient than any other known process used by other atomic powers.

If more countries — including those in Latin America — are drawn into this alliance, we shall see a formidable new political force in the world.

The paradox is that many grass roots Americans will feel more comfortable with the new Fourth World than with the Marxist-aiding elitists in the First and Second Worlds.

KISSINGER AND REAGAN

We found this report in a British journal (*Now,* September 19, 1980.) We have not seen it reported in the US that William

F. Buckley was interviewed by British columnist Geoffrey Wansell and made the following statements:

> *"He* [Buckley] *told me last week that he had just been acting as an intermediary in a series of secret negotiations betwen Ronald Reagan and former Secretary of State Henry Kissinger about the possibility of Dr. Kissinger returning to the Government* [sic] *if Reagan wins the Presidency in November."*

Which is just as we have been warning for the past year: Reagan will go along with the Trilaterals, knowingly or unknowingly.

Wansell made another statement which, if true, (Wansell has no axe to grind in US elections), strips Reagan of his conservative image:

> *"Reagan told me that once he'd put Bush on the ticket as Vice President he had to have an ideological saliva test every time he opened his mouth in case he alienated the conservatives in the Republican Party."*

STATE DEPARTMENT TAKE NOTE!

The July 1, 1980 issue of *Europa* (a supplement of the Paris publication, *Le Monde*) published an interview with South African Prime Minister Pieter W. Botha, in which he made this statement:

> *"I think a lot of hypocrisy is applied against us for international opportunist reasons to satisfy the demands of certain states. Take Miami. The most serious eruptions took place in Miami: People died in the fights that broke out. One of the black leaders in America was shot recently. Yet America has the audacity, through one of its departments, to criticize South Africa for internal problems we are experiencing in some parts of our country."*

THE UNSTABLE DEBT BALLOON

In September there was a run on Institutional Liquid Assets, the second largest money market fund catering to institutional buyers.

In an almost unheard of action, Solomon Brothers and First Chicago rescued the fund: Solomon Brothers kicked in $700,000 and First Chicago provided $1,000,000.

The fund's advisor, First Chicago, went "long and wrong" and precipitated the crisis. One fund manager commented in the October 9 *Wall Street Journal:*

> *"It's not somebody in the industry that did it. It's a bank that came in and did it to the industry. We're familiar with our business. The banks give an impression of stability and marble floors or whatever, but it's a bank that blew it."*

First Chicago is close to Chase Manhattan and is a "heavy" in the Trilateral sphere of influence. Again the question is raised: If these people can't even run their own businesses efficiently and without major disasters, how do they hope to run the economics of the world any better?

REAGAN'S EDGE

We are increasingly uneasy over Reagan's link to Trilaterals. The October 13 issue of *Newsweek* features Reagan in an AP photo with three top associates who were, according to the caption, "Thinking big."

Who were these "big thinkers" pictured with Reagan? None other than:

- **George Bush**
- **Henry Kissinger**
- Alexander Haig

Given Reagan's known preference for consensus action rather than strong-minded individual action, there is little doubt where a Reagan administration will lead us.

DAVID SPEAKS OUT

Speaking before the American Bankers Association convention in Chicago on October 13, **David Rockefeller** announced that:

- he is against inflation.
- he is against further increases in government spending.
- increases in social security should be tied to increases in hourly wages.

The assorted foundations that are controlled by such a small group of people, Rockefellers included, have been the vanguard of change over the past five decades. They have created policy, changed long-standing institutions and established new ones, all of which has led to a general public distrust of government and bureaucracy. Their policies-in-action have directly led to inflation and a bankrupt social security system.

If **David Rockefeller** is really against inflation, why doesn't he suggest that the banking system simply stop creating new money and credit?

JIM DINES MEETS HENRY K.

The original "gold bug" investment newsletter writer-adviser is Jim Dines. Jim had the opportunity to meet **Henry Kissinger** when they shared a speaker's platform at a national investment seminar.

Dines, who has a keen sense of humor, probably wanted a serious answer when he asked **Kissinger** if the Trilateral Commission was running the world — to which **Kissinger** replied:

"I am insulted. Why do I need the Trilateral Commission when I can run the world all by myself?"

FORBES PUTS IN 2 CENTS

The November 24 issue of Forbes titles their story, "What's a Trilateral Commission?" Written by Jerry Flint, this three-page editorial portrays critics of the Commission as being radicals from the far right or the far left. No one else would dare poke serious criticism at the Commission. Rather, all the "moderates" would show up the humor and folly of it all with understatement and sarcasm.

Among those critics interviewed were Laurence Shoup, author of *The Carter Presidency and Beyond.* Flint doesn't mention that Shoup is a self-acknowledged and outspoken Marxist.

On the other side was John McManus of the John Birch Society, a small, albeit vocal, minority of Trilateral critics.

Then there was Patrick Wood, who was labeled as being on

the "Right radical end of the political fringe," even to the right of the John Birch Society.

Flint brought in all the nonsense arguments: making **David Rockefeller** out to be "Dr. No" or "cabalist-in-chief," making their goal to run us into war, and even going so far as to throw in the anti-Semitic Protocols of Zion as if that were part of it too.

Take note Jerry: much of our time is spent convincing people that **Rockefeller** is *not* "Dr. No" nor "cabalist-in-chief." The anti-Semitic literature we get in the mail gets thrown in the garbage.

Flint writes:

"Alas, people and their conspiracy theories are not easily parted. It is much easier to imagine a villain than to think things through."

O.K. We have a sense of humor too. But we are sad that *you* have not thought things through.

P.S. (What's a Forbes?)

BILLIONS IN BAD DEBTS

These two stories appeared within hours of each other on our Reuter's news wire:

"Washington, Reuters — The Federal Government should take stronger action to collect debts of 175 billion dollars, the General Accounting Office said today.

"The GAO, the investigating agence of Congress, said about 25 billion dollars owed to the government is seriously delinquent and 6.3 billion dollars may have to be written off as uncollectable.

"The debts come from loans made through various programs to individuals and foreign governments."

"Washington, Reuters — The International Monetary Fund, in the largest loan it has ever made to a developing nation, is expected to approve a 1.7 billion dollar package to Pakistan, monetary sources said today.

"The loan, expected to be approved next week, comes when there is Western concern about Pakistan's stability after the

Soviet Union's military intervention in neighboring Afganistan.

"The United States had planned to give 400 million dollars worth of miltary and economic aid to Pakistan but this was rejected as not enough."

WHEAT EMBARGO SPLIT

It appears that the US has undercut Canada in selling grain to China. Canada has long sold grain to China, and considers it a "traditional" market. The US negotiated to sell up to nine million metric tons of grain a year for the next four years.

Canada has now split with the US over the Soviet grain embargo by increasing its sales target for wheat shipments to the USSR. Hence, as far as Russia is concerned, the grain embargo is effectively over.

UN ISN'T LIKED

In the opinion of the American public, the effectiveness of the United Nations has diminished in the last three years. According to Reuters, the poll was sponsored by the United Nations Association of the United States of America (UNA-USA), and showed that 53 per cent of those questioned felt the UN was doing a poor job. This is 14% higher than three years ago.

UNA-USA is a private group interested in promoting public knowledge of the UN and increasing its effectiveness. Its supporters include Rockefeller Brothers Foundation, Lilly Endowment and the Rockefeller Foundation.

The aforementioned Forbes article quoted TC Coordinator George Franklin as saying,

"We haven't a single advocate of world government." (p. 46)

Come on, George. Bending the truth is one thing, but this is an outright lie.

DAVID PACKARD TAKE NOTE

David Packard and his fellow traveling Peking traders should take note of a document published in Paris by *Le Quotidien Du Peuple* on April 28, 1980 and reproduced by *L'Express* on November 1, 1980.

The secret Chinese Communist Party document reports that the human cost of the Chinese Communist cultural revolution was 100 million dead Chinese.

We see that Western-designed factories are springing up in China to take advantage of "cheap labor" so that the multinationals can "maintain a competitive edge in the world market." What a cost to pay!

LARGEST SOVIET DEAL EVER

Russia wants to build a fourteen billion-dollar natural gas pipeline from Siberia to Western Europe. Two competitors for up to six billion dollars of this amount in equipment, tractors and parts are Caterpillar Tractor (**Robert S. Ingersoll** is a director) and Komatsu, Ltd. of Tokyo (**Kosuke Hiraoka** is a vice president).

Caterpillar seems to have the edge right now, and hopes to start things off by selling the Soviets seventy-nine million dollars worth of pipelayer tractors for the 3,000 mile project.

Does this violate US trade sanctions? No, they say. In any case, since the negotiations taking place in Moscow are between the Soviets and West Europeans, whatever is decided is completely outside the jurisdiction of the US government.

Some fear that this will ultimately lead to pressure on NATO in that Western Europe would be more dependent on Soviet energy supplies.

Our common sense tells us that the Soviets are really interested in having the ability to deliver large quantities of energy resources to Eastern Europe in case of war with Western Europe. Those who would say this deal has no military significance underestimate the intelligence of the Soviets. A hydrocarbon-fueled land force can't run on an empty tank.

ADMIRAL AND SENATOR-ELECT JEREMIAH DENTON

Jeremiah Denton is from Alabama, a newly elected Senator, a former admiral and former prisoner of war in Vietnam.

Senator-elect Denton maybe doesn't know it — but he has the opportunity to make history, an opportunity given to few other members of Congress.

Denton has the following attributes (according to our file):

- He is a Constitutional American.
- He comes to Washington, D.C. with the backing of Moral Majority and its supporters.
- He is a former admiral and prisoner of war with personal knowledge of the betrayal of American forces by our elite.

In brief, Denton is a Constitutional American disgusted at the decline (and almost fall) of the republic.

After noting the above, a minor news item caught our editorial eye.

Senator Strom Thurmond is now chairman of the Senate Judiciary Committee. In early December, Strom Thurmond announced a new senate subcommittee on security and terrorism. It will be headed by Senator-elect Jeremiah Denton.

For decades successive security committees have been blocked by the establishment when it comes to investigation of aid and comfort to our enemies from within the highest echelons of the Wall Street establishment. Let's not kid ourselves. Gus Hall and the CPUSA have miniscule influence on the United States. Our security problem is not Gus Hall but the self-perpetuating elite emanating from Wall Street. We could propose 100 topics demanding a thorough public investigation — from Pearl Harbor to our military assistance to the Soviet Union to the Trilateral Commission. Will Senator-elect Denton pick up the challenge?

MORE TRILATERAL CONFLICT OF INTEREST

As the world knows, the **Carter** family fortunes are based on government-subsidized peanuts.

There is an import quota on peanuts. The quota is small, only 1.7 million pounds per year; so, few foreign peanuts get into the US. In effect, there is an embargo on foreign peanuts.

This is causing higher peanut prices across the board, from peanut butter processors to candy store sales. Higher prices for peanuts are obviously advantageous to the **Carter** family.

President **Carter** has the power to lift the import quota with a stroke of his pen.

CENTRAL AMERICA AND THE CARIBBEAN

The **Carter** administration has almost succeeded in allowing the Soviet's Marxist allies to take over the Central American-Caribbean area.

A first-rate article surveying the tragedy of US-Soviet "cooperation" in this area with the more realistic Latin American view is in David C. Jordan's *The Turbulent Caribbean: Three Views of U.S. Policy (Strategic Review,* Fall 1980, published by United States Strategic Institute, Box 8100, Boston, MA 02114, $3.75 a single copy).

CRANSTON VS. PACKARD

Cranston and **Packard** have land interests in the Roseville, California area and **Cranston** has been using his political clout to get a highway project in the area — clear conflict of interest. It also links **Packard** and **Cranston,** supposedly poles apart politically but in fact closely allied in the internationalist first brigade.

ANDERSON CONTRIBUTIONS

If readers still consider **Packard** to be a political conservative, note that **Packard** backed Senator **Cranston** in California.

Nationally, **Packard** put money behind **John Anderson.** The Federal Election Commission printout for **Anderson** includes the following contribution:

PACKARD, DAVID   Owner Hewlett-Packard
26580 Taaffe Road
Los Altos Hills, Calif. 94022   2/04/80 $1,000.00

At a later date, TO will explore the influence of the Hoover Institution on the Reagan Administration and — more important — who is behind the Hoover Institution.

NEW YORK BANKS OVERPAID

The *Wall Street Journal* inadvertently gave a clue why New York is perpetually in financial trouble. On December 23, 1980 *WSJ* reported that NYC overpaid 10 major banks — including Chase Manhattan — some $5.5. million from 1977 to 1979.

The overpayment was subtle: non-interest-bearing accounts left with the banks in return for services, were kept unnecessarily too large. As a result, the banks had use of the extra money, interest free, and loaned it out at current rates. It netted them some extra $5.5 million in two years.

Now NYC wants "its" money back. In that we live in a "buyer beware" society, will Chase and the other nine banks be nice guys and give the money back?

Another point to investigate: did the banks have a "friend" in the NYC government who facilitated the overly large interest-free deposits? (TO is forever asking questions.)

AUTOMAKERS CONTINUE GLOBAL

Much has been said about the globalization of the auto industry. GM and Ford are hardly more American than Toyota and Datsun are German. Fiat led the consortium that delivered the blueprints to build the Kama River truck plant in the USSR.

It takes Japanese workers only thirteen hours to make a car that takes American workers thirty hours to complete. Despite the fact that Japanese cars are more expensive to American buyers, Japan for the first time has surpassed the United States in total car production by some three million units. This is no paltry amount, either.

Auto production, along with steel, is America's backbone and has been for decades. It's what made America great. Now, in a little over thirty years, Japan has built from ashes to out strip even our strong points.

On another side, Volkswagenwerk is discussing producing Volkswagen autos in Japan. (Germany also built from ashes after WW II.)

Who financed and has major control in Germany's and Japan's industrial machines?

APPENDIX B

APPENDIX B

(As of October 20, 1980)

The Trilateral Commission

GEORGES BERTHOIN *European Chairman*	TAKESHI WATANABE *Japanese Chairman*	DAVID ROCKEFELLER *North American Chairman*
EGIDIO ORTONA *European Deputy Chairman*	NOBUHIKO USHIBA *Japanese Deputy Chairman*	MITCHELL SHARP *North American Deputy Chairman*
	GEORGE S. FRANKLIN *Coordinator*	
MARTINE TRINK *European Secretary*	TADASHI YAMAMOTO *Japanese Secretary*	CHARLES B. HECK *North American Secretary*

North American Members

David M. Abshire, *Chairman, Georgetown University Center for Strategic and International Studies*

Gardner Ackley, *Henry Carter Adams University Professor of Political Economy, University of Michigan*

Graham Allison, *Dean, John F. Kennedy School of Government, Harvard University*

Doris Anderson, *President, The Canadian Advisory Council on the Status of Women; former Editor,* Châtelaine *Magazine*

John B. Anderson, *U.S. House of Representatives*

J. Paul Austin, *Chairman, The Coca-Cola Company*

Bruce Babbitt, *Governor of Arizona*

George W. Ball, *Senior Managing Director, Lehman Brothers Kuhn Loeb Incorporated; former U.S. Under Secretary of State*
Michel Belanger, *President and Chief Executive Officer, National Bank of Canad*
Lucy Wilson Benson, *Consultant and Corporate Director; former U.S. Under Secretary of State for Security, Science and Technology*
W. Michael Blumenthal, *Vice Chairman and Chief Executive Officer, Burroughs Corporation; former U.S. Secretary of the Treasury*
*Robert W. Bonner, Q.C., *Chairman, British Columbia Hydro*
Robert R. Bowie, *Harvard Center for International Affairs*
John Brademas, *U.S. House of Representatives*
Andrew Brimmer, *President, Brimmer & Company, Inc.*
John F. Burlingame, *Vice Chairman of the Board and Executive Officer, General Electric Company*
Arthur F. Burns, *Distinguished Scholar in Residence, The American Enterprise Institute for Public Policy Research; former Chairman of Board of Governors, U.S. Federal Reserve Board*
George Busbee, *Governor of Georgia*
Philip Caldwell, *Chairman of the Board, The Ford Motor Company*
Hugh Calkins, *Partner, Jones, Day, Reavis & Pogue*
Claude Castonguay, *President, Fonds Laurentien; Chairman of the Board, Imperial Life Assurance Company; former Minister in the Quebec Governmen*
Sol Chaikin, *President, International Ladies' Garment Workers' Union*
William S. Cohen, *United States Senate*
*William T. Coleman, Jr., *Senior Partner, O'Melveny & Myers; former U.S. Secretary of Transportation*
Barber B. Conable, Jr., *U.S. House of Representatives*
John Cowles, Jr., *Chairman, Minneapolis Star & Tribune Co.*
John C. Culver, *United States Senate*
Gerald L. Curtis, *Director, East Asian Institute, Columbia University*
Louis A. Desrochers, *Partner, McCuaig, Desrochers, Edmonton*
Peter Dobell, *Director, Parliamentary Centre for Foreign Affairs and Foreign Trade, Ottawa*
Thomas Donahue, *Secretary-Treasurer, AFL-CIO*
Claude A. Edwards, *Member, Public Service Staff Relations Board; former President, Public Service Alliance of Canada*
Daniel J. Evans, *President, The Evergreen State College; former Governor of Washington*
Gordon Fairweather, *Chief Commissioner, Canadian Human Rights Commission*
Thomas S. Foley, *U.S. House of Representatives*
*George S. Franklin, *Coordinator, The Trilateral Commission; former Executive Director, Council on Foreign Relations*
John Allen Fraser, *Member of Canadian Parliament*
John H. Glenn, Jr., *United States Senate*
Walter A. Haas, Jr., *Chairman, Levi Strauss Company*
Donald Southam Harvie, *Deputy Chairman, Petro Canada*
Philip M. Hawley, *President, Carter Hawley Hale Stores, Inc.*
Walter W. Heller, *Regents' Professor of Economics, University of Minnesota*

William A. Hewitt, *Chairman, Deere & Company*
Carla A. Hills, *Senior Resident Partner, Latham, Watkins & Hills; former U.S. Secretary of Housing and Urban Development*
Alan Hockin, *Executive Vice President, Toronto-Dominion Bank*
James F. Hoge, Jr., *Publisher,* Chicago Sun Times
Hendrik S. Houthakker, *Henry Lee Professor of Economics, Harvard University*
Thomas L. Hughes, *President, Carnegie Endowment for International Peace*
*Robert S. Ingersoll, *U.S. Chairman, Japan-U.S. Economic Relations Group; former U.S. Deputy Secretary of State and Ambassador to Japan*
D. Gale Johnson, *Provost, The University of Chicago*
Edgar F. Kaiser, Jr., *President and Chief Executive Officer, Kaiser Resources Ltd., Vancouver, and Kaiser Steel Company, Oakland*
Lane Kirkland, *President, AFL-CIO*
*Henry A. Kissinger, *Former U.S. Secretary of State*
Joseph Kraft, *Columnist*
Juanita Kreps, *Former U.S. Secretary of Commerce*
Sol M. Linowitz, *Senior Partner, Coudert Brothers; U.S. Ambassador to Mideast Autonomy Negotiations*
Winston Lord, *President, Council on Foreign Relations*
Donald S. Macdonald, *McCarthy & McCarthy; former Canadian Minister of Finance*
*Bruce K. MacLaury, *President, The Brookings Institution*
Paul W. McCracken, *Edmund Ezra Day Professor of Business Administration, University of Michigan*
Darcy McKeough, *President and Chief Executive Officer, Union Gas, Ltd., Chatham, Ontario*
Arjay Miller, *Dean Emeritus, Graduate School of Business, Stanford University*
Kenneth D. Naden, *President, National Council of Farmer Cooperatives*
Joseph S. Nye, Jr., *John F. Kennedy School of Government, Harvard University*
David Packard, *Chairman, Hewlett-Packard Company*
Gerald L. Parsky, *Partner, Gibson, Dunn & Crutcher; former U.S. Assistant Secretary of the Treasury for International Affairs*
William R. Pearce, *Vice President, Cargill Incorporated*
Peter G. Peterson, *Chairman, Lehman Brothers Kuhn Loeb Incorporated*
Edwin O. Reischauer, *University Professor and Director of Japan Institute, Harvard University; former U.S. Ambassador to Japan*
John E. Rielly, *President, The Chicago Council on Foreign Relations*
*Charles W. Robinson, *Chairman, Energy Transition Corporation; former U.S. Deputy Secretary of State*
*David Rockefeller, *Chairman, The Chase Manhattan Bank, N.A.*
John D. Rockefeller, IV, *Governor of West Virginia*
Robert V. Roosa, *Partner, Brown Bros., Harriman & Company*
*William M. Roth, *Roth Properties*
William V. Roth, Jr., *United States Senate*
Henry B. Schacht, *Chairman, Cummins Engine Inc.*
J. Robert Schaetzel, *Former U.S. Ambassador to the European Communities*
William W. Scranton, *Former Governor of Pennsylvania; former U.S. Ambassador to the United Nations*

Elliot L. Richardson, *U.S. Ambassador at Large with Responsibility for UN Law of the Sea Conference*
John C. Sawhill, *Chairman, U.S. Synthetic Fuels Corporation*
Gerard C. Smith, *U.S. Ambassador at Large for Non-Proliferation Matters*
Paul A. Volcker, *Chairman, Board of Governors, U.S. Federal Reserve System*

Unlisted Former Members

I. W. Abel, *Former President, United Steelworkers*
Ernest C. Arbuckle, *Chairman, Saga Corporation*
Anne Armstrong, *Former U.S. Ambassador to Great Britain*
Russell Bell, *Director, Canadian Labor Congress*
C. Fred Bergsten, *Former Deputy Under Secretary of the Treasury*
Bernard Bonin, *Director, Institute of Applied Economics, Ecole des hautes etudes commerciales, Canada*
William Brock, *Former Chairman, Republican National Committee*
George Bush, *Vice President of the United States*
Alden W. Clausen, President, Bank of America
Alan Cranston, *United States Senate*
John C. Danforth, *United States Senate*
Archibald K. Davis, *Former Chairman, Wachovia Bank & Trust Co.*
Emmett Dedmon, *Former Vice-President & Editorial Director, Field Enterprises, Inc.*
Brian Flemming, *Stuart MacKee & Covert, Halifax*
Donald M. Fraser, *Mayor of Minneapolis*
Patrick Haggerty, *Honorary Chairman, Texas Instruments, Inc.*
John K. Jamieson, *Former Chairman & CEO, Exxon Corporation*
Clause Masson, *Director, Division of Planning & Research, Department of Trade & Commerce, Ottawa*
Lee L. Morgan, *Chairman, Caterpillar Tractor Company*
F. R. Murray, *Former Director, Hudson Company*
Jean-Luc Pepin, *Former Chairman of the Anti-Inflation Board of Canada*
John H. Perkins, *President, Continental Illinois National Bank & Trust Co.*
Anthony M. Solomon, *Former Under Secretary of the Treasury for Monetary Affairs*
Maurice F. Strong, *Former Chairman, Petro Canada; Chairman, AZL Resources, Inc.*
Cyrus Vance, *Former U.S. Secretary of State*
Arthur M. Wood, *Former Chairman, Sears, Roebuck & Co.*
Leonard Woodcock, *U.S. Ambassador to the People's Republic of China*

European Members

*Giovanni Agnelli, *President, FIAT*
*P. Nyboe Andersen, *Chief General Manager, Andelsbanken A / S; former Danish Minister for Economic Affairs and Trade*
Luis Maria Anson, *Presidente de la Agencia EFE, Madrid; Presidente, Federacion Nacional de Asociaciones de la Prensa*
Giovanni Auletta Armenise, *Chairman, Banca Nazionale dell'Agricoltura, Rome*
Piero Bassetti, *Chamber of Deputies, Rome*
E. K. den Bakker, *Chairman of the Board, Nationale Nederlanden*
*Georges Berthoin, *President, European Movement*
Kurt H. Biedenkopf, *Deputy Chairman, Christian Democratic Union, Federal Republic of Germany; Member of the Bundestag*
Kurt Birrenbach, *Presidmnt, German Foreign Policy Association*
Claudio Boada Villalonga, *Chairman, Banco de Madrid; former Chairman, Instituto Nacional de Industria, Madrid*
Marcel Boiteux, *Chairman, French Electricity Board*
*Henrik N. Boon, *Chairman, Netherlands Institute for International Affairs; former Dutch Ambassador to NATO and Italy*
Guido Carli, *President, Confindustria; former Governor, Bank of Italy*
Hervé de Carmoy, *General Manager, Midland Bank, London; Chief Executive Officer, BCT, Midland Bank, Paris*
Jaime Carvajal, *Chairman, Banco Urquijo, Madrid*
Jean Claude Casanova, *Conseiller auprès du Premièr Ministre; former Professor of Political Science, Institute of Political Studies, Paris*
José Luis Cerón, *Former President of the Spanish Board of Trade; Chairman of ASETA*
Guido de Clercq, *General Director, Catholic University of Louvain, Belgium*
Willy de Clercq, *Chairman, Party for Freedom and Progress, Belgium; Member of European Parliament*
Umberto Colombo, *President, National Committee for Nuclear Energy, Rome*
Guido Colonna di Paliano, *Former Italian Ambassador to Norway; former Member of the Commission of the European Communities*
Richard Conroy, *Member of Senate, Irish Republic*
Antoinette Danis-Spaak, *Chairman, Democratic Front of French Speaking Bruxellois; Member of Chamber of Representatives; Member of European Parliament*
*Paul Delouvrier, *Président de l'Etablissement Public Chargé de l'Aménagemen du Parc de la Villette; former Chairman, French Electricity Board*
Geoffrey Drain, *General Secretary of the National Association for Local Government Offices (NALGO), London*
Jean Dromer, *Président Directeur Général, Banque Internationale pour l'Afrique Occidentale*
François Duchêne, *Director, Sussex European Research Centre, University of Sussex*
*Horst Ehmke, *Deputy Chairman, Parliamentary Fraction of Social Democrati Party, Federal Republic of Germany; Member of the Bundestag; former Minister of Justice*

Pierre Esteva, *Président, Union des Assurances de Paris*

*Carlos Ferrer, *Chairman, Spanish Confederation of Employers' Organizations; Chairman, Ferrer International*

K. Fibbe, *Chairman of the Board, Overseas Gas and Electricity Company, Rotterdam*

*Garret FitzGerald, *Member of Irish Parliament and Leader of Fine Gael Party; former Foreign Minister of Ireland*

René Foch, *Conseiller au Parti Républicain sur les Questions Internationales*

Antonio Garrigues, *Chairman, Asociación para el Progreso de la Dirección, Madrid*

*Michel Gaudet, *Président, Fédération Française des Sociétés d'Assurances; Président du Comité Européen des Assurances*

Giuseppe Glisenti, *Vice President, Invest, S.P.A., Milan*

Hans Hartwig, *Chairman, German Association for Wholesale and Foreign Trade*

Denis Healey, *Member of British Parliament; former Chancellor of the Exchequer*

Edward Heath, *Member of British Parliament; former Prime Minister*

Terence Higgins, *Member of British Parliament; former Minister of State and Financial Secretary to the Treasury*

Diether Hoffman, *Member of Board of Directors, Bank für Gemeinwirtschaft A.G., Frankfurt / Main*

Josef P. Houthuys, *Chairman, Belgian Confederation of Christian Trade Unions*

Ludwig Huber, *President, Bayerische Landesbank, Girozentrale Munich*

Horst K. Jannot, *Chairman, Board of Directors, Munich Reinsurance Society*

Daniel E. Janssen, *Director-General, Belgian Chemical Union*

Karl Kaiser, *Director, Research Institute of the German Society for Foreign Policy*

Lord Keith of Castleacre, *Member, British House of Lords; former Chairman, Rolls Royce Ltd.*

Henry N. L. Keswick, *Chairman, Matheson & Company Ltd.*

Michael Killeen, *Managing Director, Industrial Development Authority of the Irish Republic*

Norbert Kloten, *President, Central Bank of State of Baden-Württemberg*

*Max Kohnstamm, *President, European University Institute, Florence*

Erwin Kristoffersen, *Director, International Division, German Federation of Trade Unions*

Jacques Lallement, *Directeur Général du Crédit Agricole, Paris*

Baron Léon Lambert, *Président du Groupe Bruxelles Lambert, S.A.*

Liam Lawlor, *Member of Irish Parliament*

Arrigo Levi, *Columnist, La Stampa, Turin, and The Times, London*

Mark Littman, *Queen's Counsel, Rio-Tinto Zinc Corporation Ltd., London*

Richard Löwenthal, *Professor Emeritus, Free University of Berlin*

Francisco Lucas Pires, *Vice President, Central Social Democratic Party (CDS), Portugal*

Evan Luard, *Former Parliamentary Undersecretary of State for the British Foreign Office*

*Roderick MacFarquhar, *Former Member of British Parliament*

*Carlos March Delgado, *Chairman, Banca March, Madrid; Vice Chairman, Juan March Foundation*

Robert Marjolin, *Former Vice President of the Commision of the European Communities*

Roger Martin, *Former President, Compagnie Saint Gobain Pont-à-Mousson*

Hanns W. Maull, *Editor, Bayerischer Rundfunk; European Director, Japan Ce for International Exchange*

Pietro Merli-Brandini, *Secretary General, Italian Confederation of Free Trade Unions*

Cesare Merlini, *Director, Institute for International Affairs, Rome*

Thierry de Montbrial, *Professor, Ecole Polytechnique; Director, Institut Franç des Relations Internationales, Paris*

Alwin Münchmeyer, *Chairman of the Board, Bank Schröder, Münchmeyer, Hengst & Co.*

Preben Munthe, *Professor of Economics, Oslo University; Official Chief Negotiator in Negotiations between Labor Unions and Industry*

Dan Murphy, *Secretary-General of the Civil Service Executive Union, Dublin*

*Karl-Heinz Narjes, *Member of the Bundestag*

Friedrich A. Neuman, *Chairman, State Association, Industrial Employers Societies, North-Rhine Westphalia*

*Egidio Ortona, *President, Honeywell Information Systems, Italia; former Italian Ambassador to the United States*

Alfonso Osorio, *Member of Spanish House of Representatives; former Vice President of the Spanish Government*

David Owen, *Member of British Parliament; former Secretary of State for Foreign and Commonwealth Affairs*

Bernard Pagezy, *Président Directeur Général, Sociétés des Assurances du Groupe de Paris*

Antonio Pedrol, *Chairman, Consejo General de la Abogacía Española*

Sir John Pilcher, *Director of the Foreign and Colonial Investment Trust; former British Ambassador to Japan*

Paulo de Pitta e Cunha, *Professor, Department of Economics, Faculty of La University of Lisbon; Chairman, Portuguese Association for the Study of European Integration*

Konrad Porzner, *Parlamentarischer Geschaeftsfuehrer der Sozialdemokratischen Bundestagsfraktion; Member of the Bundestag*

Jean Rey, *Ministre d'Etat, Belgium; Member of European Parliament; former President of the Commission of the European Communities*

Julian Ridsdale, *Member of British Parliament; Chairman, Anglo-Japanese Parliamentary Group*

Sir Frank Roberts, *Director, Mercedes Benz, U.K. and Hoechst, U.K.; former British Ambassador to Germany, the Soviet Union, and NATO*

Lord Roll of Ipsden, *Chairman, S. G. Warburg and Co. Ltd.*

John Roper, *Member of British Parliament*

François de Rose, *Ambassadeur de France; Président Directeur Général, Société Nouvelle Pathé Cinéma*

Baron Edmond de Rothschild, *Président, Compagnie Financière Holding, Pa*

Ivo Samkalden, *Former Mayor of Amsterdam*

Viscount Sandon, *Deputy Chairman, National Westminster Bank Limited; Chairman, Orion Bank Limited*

John C. Sanness, *Professor, Norwegian Institute for Foreign Affairs*
W. E. Scherpenhuijsen Rom, *Chairman, Board of Managing Directors, Nederlandsche Middenstandsbank, N.V.*
Erik Ib Schmidt, *Permanent Undersecretary of State, Denmark; Chairman, Risø National Laboratory*
Th. M. Scholten, *Chairman of the Board, Robeco Investment Group, Rotterdam*
Gerhard Schröder, *Member of the Bundestag; former Foreign Minister of the Federal Republic of Germany*
Pedro Schwartz, *Director, Instituto de Económia de Mercado, Madrid*
José Antonio Segurado, *Chairman, International Relations Commission, Spanish Confederation of Employers' Organizations; Chairman, SEFISA*
Erik Seidenfaden, *Editor; Directeur de la Fondation Danoise, Institut Universitaire International de Paris*
Federico Sensi, *Ambassador of Italy; former Italian Ambassador to the Soviet Union*
Roger Seydoux, *Ambassadeur de France; Président du Conseil d'Administration, Fondation de France*
Lord Shackleton, *Deputy Chairman, Rio Tinto-Zinc Corporation Ltd., London; former Cabinet Minister*
Sir Andrew Shonfield, *Professor of Economics, European University Institute, Florence; former Director, Royal Institute of International Affairs*
*Henri Simonet, *Former Belgian Minister of Foreign Affairs*
J. H. Smith, *Deputy Chairman and Chief Executive, British Gas Corporation*
Hans-Günther Sohl, *Chairman of the Board, Thyssen A.G.*
Theo Sommer, *Editor-in-Chief,* Die Zeit
Myles Staunton, *Member of Senate, Irish Republic*
John A. Swire, *Chairman, John Swire and Sons Group of Companies*
Peter Tapsell, *Member of British Parliament; former Junior Conservative Spokesman on Foreign and Commonwealth Affairs; former Conservative Spokesman on Treasury and Economic Affairs*
Niels Thygesen, *Professor of Economics, Economic Institute, Copenhagen University*
*Otto Grieg Tidemand, *Shipowner; former Norwegian Minister of Defense and Minister of Economic Affairs*
Sir Anthony Tuke, *Chairman, Barclays Bank Ltd.*
Sir Mark Turner, *Chairman, Rio Tinto-Zinc Corporation Ltd.*
António Vasco de Mello, *Chairman of the Board, Companhia Portuguêsa de Trefilaria, SARL; President, Confederation of Portuguese Industry*
Heinz-Oskar Vetter, *Chairman, German Federation of Trade Unions; Member of European Parliament*
José Vilá Marsans, *Chairman, Sociedad Anónima de Fibras Artificiales; Director, Banco Central, Barcelona*
Paolo Vittorelli, *Member of Italian Parliament; Director,* Avanti
Sir Frederick Warner, *Chairman, Guinness Peat International Ltd; Member of European Parliament; former British Ambassador to Japan*
Luc Wauters, *Chairman, Groupe Almanij-Kredietbank, Brussels*
Edmund Wellenstein, *Former Director General for External Affairs, Commission of the European Communities*

T. Kenneth Whitaker, *Member of Senate, Irish Republic; former Governor of the Central Bank of Ireland*
Alan Lee Williams, *Director-General, English Speaking Union; former Member of British Parliament*
*Otto Wolff von Amerongen, *President, Otto Wolff A.G.; President, German Federation of Trade and Industry*
*Sir Philip de Zulueta, *Chairman, Antony Gibbs Holding, Ltd.*

*Executive Committee

Former Members in Public Service

Svend Auken, *Minister of Labor, Denmark*
Raymond Barre, *Prime Minister, French Republic*
Lord Carrington, *British Secretary of State for Foreign and Commonwealth Affairs*
Francesco Compagna, *Italian Minister of Merchant Marine*
Michel Debatisse, *Secretary of State for Agro-Food Industries, French Republic*
Herbert Ehrenberg, *Minister of Labor and Social Affairs, Federal Republic of Germany*
Marc Eyskens, *Belgian Minister of Finance*
Bernard Hayhoe, *Parliamentary Under Secretary of State in the British Defense Ministry*
Otto Graf Lambsdorff, *Minister of Economics, Federal Republic of Germany*
Jean-Philippe Lecat, *Minister of Culture and Communications, French Republi*
Giorgio La Malfa, *Italian Minister of the Budget*
Ivar Nørgaard, *Danish Minister of Environment*
Michael O'Kennedy, *Minister for Finance, Irish Republic*
Thorvald Stoltenberg, *Secretary of State, Norwegian Ministry of Foreign Affairs*
Olaf Sund, *Senator for Labor and Social Affairs, Land Government of Berlin*
Ramón Trias Fargas, *Minister of Economy and Finance, Catalan Government*
Michael Woods, *Minister for Health and Social Welfare, Irish Republic*

Unlisted Former Members

Franco Bobba, *Former Director General, Economic and Financial Affairs, Europe Economic Community*
Frederick H. Boland, *Chairman, IBM Ireland, Ltd.; former President, UN General Assembly*
Rene Bonety, *Advisor, Economic Research Department, French Electricity Board*
Michel Crepeau, *President, French Movement of Radicals of the Left*
Earl of Cromer, *Advisor, Baring Brothers & Co., Ltd.; former British Ambassador United States*
Barry Desmond, *Member of Irish Parliament; Labor Party Whip*
Fritz Dietz, *President, German Association for Wholesale and Foreign Trade*
Werner Dollinger, *Member of the Bundestag*

George G. Eastwood, *Former General Secretary, Printing and Kindred Trades Association, United Kingdom*

Max H. Fisher, *Editor, Financial Times, London*

Francesco Forte, *Professor of Financial Sciences, University of Turin*

Jacques du Fouchier, *French Secretary of State to the Minister of Agriculture*

Sir Reay Geddes, *Honorary President, Dunlop Holdings, Ltd.*

Olivier Giscard d'Estaing, *Administrator, IBM; brother of the President, French Republic*

Ronald Grierson, *Director, General Electric Co., Ltd., London*

Lord Harlech, *Chairman, Harlech Television; former British Ambassador to the United States*

Karl Hauenschild, *Chairman, German Union of Chemical, Paper and Ceramic Workers*

Hans-Juergen Junghans, *Member of the Bundestag; Director, Salzgitter AG*

Sir Arthur Knight, *Chairman, Courtaulds, Ltd.*

Eugen Loderer, *Chairman, German Union of Metal Workers; Director, Volkswagenwerk AG*

John Loudon, *Former Chairman, Royal Dutch Shell Group & Shell Oil Co. USA*

Reginald Maudling, *Former British Chancellor of the Exchequer*

F. S. McFadzean, *Managing Director, Royal Dutch Shell Group*

Sir Con O'Neill, *Former British Ambassador to the European Economic Community; Director, Unigate, Ltd.*

Manuel de Prado y Colon, *Former Vice President, Spanish Government*

Mary T. W. Robinson, *Member of Senate, Irish Republic*

Claudio Segre, *President, Compagnie Europeenne de Placements*

G. R. Storry, *Professor, St. Anthony's College, Oxford (Far East Centre)*

Japanese Members

Isao Amagi, *Director General, Japan Society for the Promotion of Science; Advisor to the Ministry of Education*
Yoshiya Ariyoshi, *Board Counsellor, Nippon Yusen, K.K.*
Shizuo Asada, *President, Japan Air Lines Company, Ltd.*
Yoshishige Ashihara, *Chairman, Board of Directors, Kansai Electric Power Company, Inc.*
Toshiwo Doko, *Former Chairman, Japan Federation of Economic Organizatio (Keidanren); Counsellor, Toshiba Corporation*
Jun Eto, *Professor, Tokyo Institute of Technology*
Shinkichi Eto, *Professor of International Relations, Tokyo University*
*Chujiro Fujino, *Chairman, Mitsubishi Corporation*
Shintaro Fukushima, *Chairman, Kyodo News Service*
Noboru Gotoh, *Chairman and President, TOKYU Corporation* .
Nihachiro Hanamura, *Executive Vice Chairman and President, Japan Federati of Economic Organizations (Keidanren)*
Sumio Hara, *Executive Advisor, Bank of Tokyo, Ltd.*
Norishige Hasegawa, *Chairman, Sumitomo Chemical Company, Ltd.*
Teru Hidaka, *Director and Senior Counsellor, Yamaichi Securities Company, I*
Kosuke Hiraoka, *Vice President, Komatsu, Ltd.*
Gen Hirose, *President, Nihon Life Insurance Co., Ltd.*
Hideo Hori, *President, The National Association for Employment for the Handicapped*
*Takashi Hosomi, *Advisor, The Industrial Bank of Japan, Ltd.*
Hosai Hyuga, *Chairman of the Board, Sumitomo Metal Industries, Ltd.*
Shinichi Ichimura, *Professor of Economics, Kyoto University*
Yoshizo Ikeda, *Chairman, Mitsui & Co., Ltd.*
Yoshihiro Inayama, *Chairman, Japan Federation of Economic Organizations (Keidanren); Representative Director, Chairman of the Board, Nippon Steel Corporation*
Kaoru Inouye, *Chairman of the Senior Executive Committee, Dai-Ichi Kangyo Bank, Ltd.*
Rokuro Ishikawa, *President, Kajima Corporation*
Tadao Ishikawa, *President, Keio University*
Joji Itakura, *Counsellor, The Mitsui Bank, Ltd.*
Yoshizane Iwasa, *Counsellor, Fuji Bank, Ltd.; Chairman, Japan-U.S. Economic Council*
Motoo Kaji, *Professor of Economics, Tokyo University*
Fuji Kamiya, *Professor of International Relations, Keio University*
*Yusuke Kashiwagi, *President, Bank of Tokyo, Ltd.; former Special Advisor to the Minister of Finance*
Koichi Kato, *Member of the Diet; former Deputy Chief Cabinet Secretary*
Katsuji Kawamata, *Chairman, Nissan Motor Company, Ltd.*
Kiichiro Kitaura, *Chairman, Nomura Securities Company, Ltd.*
Koji Kobayashi, *Chairman of the Board, Chief Executive Officer, Nippon Electric Company, Ltd.*

Yotaro Kobayashi, *President, Fuji-Xerox*
Shinichi Kondo, *Advisor to the Board of Directors, Mitsubishi Corporation;
  former Ambassador to Canada*
Fumihiko Kono, *Counsellor, Mitsubishi Heavy Industries, Ltd.*
Masataka Kosaka, *Professor, Faculty of Law, Kyoto University*
Fumihiko Maki, *Principal, Maki and Associates, Design, Planning and
  Development*
Shigeharu Matsumoto, *Chairman, International House of Japan, Inc.*
Daigo Miyado, *Chairman of the Board, The Sanwa Bank, Ltd.*
Akio Morita, *Chairman, Representative Managing Director, SONY Corporation*
Takashi Mukaibo, *President, Tokyo University*
Norihiko Nagai, *Chairman, Mitsui O.S.K. Lines, Ltd.*
Yonosuke Nagai, *Professor of Political Science, Tokyo Institute of Technology*
Shigeo Nagano, *Honorary Chairman, Nippon Steel Corporation; President,
  Japan Chamber of Commerce and Industry*
Eiichi Nagasue, *Member of the Diet*
Nobuyuki Nakahara, *Managing Director, Toa Nenryo Kogyo, K.K.*
Toshio Nakamura, *Chairman, Mitsubishi Bank, Ltd.*
Sohei Nakayama, *Counsellor, The Industrial Bank of Japan, Ltd.*
Akira Ogata, *Advisor to the Chief News Commentator, Japan Broadcasting
  Corporation (NHK)*
Toshihisa Ohjimi, *President, Arabian Oil Company, Ltd.; former Vice Minister
  of International Trade and Industry*
Kazuo Oikawa, *General President, Japan Telecommunications Workers' Union
  (Zendentsu); Vice Chairman, General Council of Trade Unions of Japan
  (SOHYO)*
Saburo Okita, *Former Minister of Foreign Affairs*
Keiichi Oshima, *Professor of Nuclear Engineering, Tokyo University*
Kiichi Saeki, *Chairman, Nomura Research Institute*
Kunihiko Sasaki, *Director, Honorary Chairman, Fuji Bank, Ltd.*
Yukio Shibayama, *Chairman, Sumitomo Corporation*
Masahide Shibusawa, *Director, East-West Seminar*
Toshihito Shimada, *President, Takahashi Foundation; former President,
  Japan Petroleum Development Corporation*
Ichiro Shioji, *President, Confederation of Japan Automobile Workers' Union
  (Jidosha-Soren)*
Tatsuo Shoda, *Chairman of the Board, The Nippon Credit Bank, Ltd.*
Sinsuke Sugiura, *Chairman, The Long Term Credit Bank of Japan, Ltd.*
Chusuke Takahashi, *Executive Vice President, The Sumitomo Bank*
Ryuji Takeuchi, *Advisor to the Minister for Foreign Affairs; former
  Ambassador to the United States*
Eiji Toyoda, *President, Toyota Motor Company, Ltd.*
Meiki Tozaki, *President, C. Itoh & Co., Ltd.*
Seiji Tsutsumi, *Chairman, Seibu Department Store, Inc.*
Tadao Umesao, *Director, National Museum of Ethnology*
Nobuhiko Ushiba, *Advisor to Minister for Foreign Affairs; Japan Chairman of
  the Japan-U.S. Economic Relations Group*
Shogo Watanabe, *Chairman, Nikko Securities Company, Ltd.*
Takeshi Watanabe, *Former President, Asian Development Bank*

Toshihiko Yamashita, *President, Matsushita Electric Industrial Co., Ltd.*
Kizo Yasui, *Senior Advisor, Toray Industries, Inc.*
Hirokichi Yoshiyama, *President, Hitachi, Ltd.*
*Executive Committee

Former Members in Public Service

Kiichi Miyazawa, *Minister of State, Chief Cabinet Secretary*

Unlisted Former Members

Toru Hagiwara, *Former Advisor to the Japanese Minister of Foreign Affairs*
Yukitaki Haraguchi, *Chairman, Central Executive Committee, All Japan Federatio*
Metal Mine Labor Unions
Yoshio Hayashi, *Member of the Japanese Diet*
Kazushige Hirasawa, *News Commentator, Japan Broadcasting Corporation*
Teizi Horikoshi, *Vice President, Japan Federation of Economic Organizations*
(Keidanren)
Shozo Hotta, *Honorary Chairman, Sumitomo Bank, Ltd.*
Hiroki Imazato, *President, Nippon Seiko K.K.*
Ryoichi Kawai, *President, Komatsu, Ltd.*
Kazutaka Kikawada, *President, Tokyo Electric Power*
Kenichiro Komai, *Chairman, Hitachi, Ltd.*
Masaharu Matsushita, *President, Matsushita Electric*
Kinhide Mushakoji, *Director, Institute of International Relations, University of So*
Tokyo
Ichiro Nakayama, *President, Japan Institute of Labor*
Kiichiro Sato, *Counselor, Mitsui Bank*
Toshisuke Sugiura, *President, The Long Term Credit Bank of Japan, Ltd.*
Kogoro Uemura, *President, Japan Federation of Economic Organizations (Keidanr*
Jiro Ushio, *President, Ushio Electric*
Eme Yamashita, *Former Vice Minister of MITI*
Kizo Yasui, *Chairman, Toray Industries, Inc.*

Note: This is the status of these individuals according to our current research.

APPENDIX C

APPENDIX C

THE TRIANGLE PAPERS

Reports of Task Forces to the Trilateral Commission
1. *Towards a Renovated World Monetary System* (1973) Rapporteurs: Richard N. Cooper, Motoo Kaji, Claudio Segre
2. *The Crisis of International Cooperation* (1974) Rapporteurs: Francois Duchene, Kinhide Mushakoji, Henry D. Owen
3. *A Turning Point in North-South Economic Relations* (1974) Rapporteurs: Richard N. Gardner, Saburo Okita, B.J. Udink
4. *Directions for World Trade in the Nineteen Seventies* (1974) Rapporteurs: Guido Colonna di Paliano, Philip H. Trezise, Nobuhiko Ushiba
5. *Energy: The Imperative for a Trilateral Approach* (1974) Rapporteurs: John C. Campbell, Herve de Carmoy, Shinichi Kondo
6. *Energy: A Strategy for International Action* (1974) Rapporteurs: John C. Campbell, Herve de Carmoy, Shinichi Kondo

7. *OPEC, the Trilateral World, and the Developing Countries: New Arrangements for Cooperation, 1976-1980* (1975)
   Rapporteurs: Richard N. Gardner, Saburo Okita, B.J. Udink

8. *The Crisis of Democracy* (1975)
   Rapporteurs: Michel Crozier, Samuel P. Huntington, Joji Watanuki

9. *A New Regime for the Oceans* (1976)
   Rapporteurs: Micheal Hardy, Ann L. Hollick, Johan Jorgen Holst, Douglas M. Johnston, Shigeru Oda

10. *Seeking a New Accomodation in World Commodity Markets* (1976)
    Rapporteurs: Carl E. Beigie, Wolfgang Hagar, Sueco Sekinguchi

11. *The Reform of International Institutions* (1976)
    Rapporteurs: C. Fred Bergsten, Georges Berthoin, Kinhide Mushakoji

12. *The Problem of International Consultations* (1976)
    Rapporteurs: Egidio Ortona, J. Robert Schaetzel, Nobuhiko Ushiba

13. *Collaboration with Communist Countries in Managing Global Problems: An Examination of the Options* (1977)
    Rapporteurs: Chihiro Hosoya, Henry D. Owen, Sir Andrew Shonfield

14. *Towards a Renovated International System* (1977)
    Rapporteurs: Richard N. Cooper, Karl Kaiser, Masataka Kosaka

15. *An Overview of East-West Relations* (1978)
    Rapporteurs: Jeremy R. Azrael, Richard Lowenthal, Tohru Nakagawa

16. *Expanding Food Production in Developing Countries: Rice Production in South and Southeast Asia* (1978)
    Rapporteurs: Umberto Colombo, D. Gale Johnson, Toshio Shishido

17. *Energy: Managing the Transition* (1978)
    Rapporteurs: John C. Sawhill, Keichi Oshima, Hanns W. Maull

18. *Collective Bargaining and Employee Participation in Western Europe, North America and Japan* (1979)
    Rapporteurs: Benjamin C. Roberts, Hideaki Okamoto, George C. Lodge
19. *Industrial Policy and the International Economy* (1979)
    Rapporteurs: John Pinder,Takashi Hosomi, William Diebold.
20. *Major Payments Imbalances and International Financial Stability* (1980)
    Rapporteurs: Masao Fujioka, Alexandre Lamfalussy, Bruce K. MacLaury
21. *North-South Trade* (1980)
    Rapporteurs: Albert Fishlow, Sueo Sekiguchi, Jean Carriere
22. *Employment, Technological Progress and Industrial Change*
    Rapporteurs: Heinz Markmann, Tadashi Hanami, Richard Nelson

Trialogue, quarterly report on Commission activities and developments. Subscription available: $10 for one year and $18 for two years.

Above material available from following address:
Trilateral Commission
North American Office
345 East 46th Street
New York, NY 10017
(212) 661-1180

BIBLIOGRAPHY

For books published by the Trilateral Commission see Appendix C.

Allen, Gary. *They Run America.* American Opinion, May and June 1978.

Allen, Gary. *They're Catching On.* American Opinion, November 1977.

Anderson, Jack, Associated Press, February 8, 1980

Associated Press, (Taipei, Taiwan), December 24, 1979.

Becker, James, editor. *Schooling for a Global Age.* New York: McGraw-Hill Book Company, 1979.

British War Cabinet Papers, 24/49/7197 Secret, April 24, 1918.

Brzezinski, Zbigniew. Washington Star, December 31, 1978, p. E4.

Brzezinski, Zbigniew. *Between Two Ages: America's Role in the Technetronic Era.* England: Penguin Books, 1976.

Buchen, Irving. *Learning for Tomorrow.* New York: Vintage Books, 1974.

Burke, Edmund. *Letter to William Smith*. Bartlett's Familiar Quotations. Boston: Little, Brown and Company, 1968.

Casserly, J.J.. *Bank Chief to Lead Regional Council,* Arizona Republic, December 6, 1980

Chadwick, Michael Loyd, editor. *The Trilateral Commission,* Freeman Digest, February/ March 1979.

Chadwick Micheal Loyd, editor. *The Aspen Institute for Humnistic Studies,* Freeman Diegest, January 1979.

Cleveland, Harlan. *The Third Try at World Order*. New York: Aspen Institute, 1976.

Cornell, George W. Associate Press Report, Arizona Republic, March 10, 1979.

Cornell, George W. Associated Press Report, Arizona Republic, March 9, 1979.

Crozier, Michael and et al. *The Crisis of Democracy*. New York: New York University Press, 1975.

Deming, Angus. *Foreign Policy: Mandarins In Trouble.* Newsweek, March 28, 1977.

Dewey, John et al. *Humanist Manifesto I and II*. New York: Prometheus Books, 1977.

Dornan, Robert K.. *Banking Interests In Panama.* Congressional Record, September 15, 1977.

Edwards, Paul. *Encyclopedia of Philosophy*. New York: Cromwell Collier and MacMillian, Inc., 1967.

El Paso Times, April 27, 1978.

FitzGerald, Garret. *"Political Cooperation: Toward a Common EEC Foreign Policy."* European Community: Commission of the European Communities, September-October 1978.

Flint, Jerry. *What's a Trilateral Commission?,* Forbes, Volume 126, Number 11 (November 24, 1980).

Gallagher, Jim. *Bryant Grinder Case.* Chicago Tribune, April 6, 1980.

Gelman, Eric. *The Great American Salon,* Newsweek, July 14, 1980.

Irvine, Reed. *Behind the News,* Washington D.C.: Accuracy In Media, 1978.

Jefferson, Thomas. *The Writings of Thomas Jefferson,* vol. 7.

Washington D.C.: Committee of Congress, 1861.

Johnson, W.A.. Daily News Digest, July 4, 1980.

Karpel, Craig S.. *Cartergate: The Death of Democracy,* Penthouse, 5 part November 1977 thru April 1978.

Kirchhoff, Dr. J.. *Corporate Missionary: those who believe in Capitalism must fight back,* Barrons, February 19, 1979.

Kitchen, Helen. *Africa: From Mystery To Maze.* Critical Choices for Americans Volume XI. New York: Lexington Books, 1976.

LaHaye, Tim. *The Battle for the Mind.* New Jersey: Fleming H. Revell Co., 1980.

Lamont, Corliss. *The Philosophy of Humanism,* 5th edition. New York: Unger, 1965.

McNellis, Maryanne. *Japan's Push for a Pacific Community,* Business Week, February 25, 1980.

Morris, Barbara, *Change Agents In the Schools.* California: Barbara M. Morris Report, 1979.

New York Times, June 12, 1921, p. 2 col. 3.

Pittman, John. *Trilateralism — U.S. Imperialism's New Scenario,* World Marxist Review, May 1978.

Protagoras. *Protagoras IX.* Bartlett's Familiar Quotations. Boston: Little, Brown and Company, 1968.

Quigley, Carroll. *Tragedy and Hope.* New York: MacMillian Company, 1966.

Rand, Ayn. *Anthem.* Idaho: The Caxton Printers, Ltd., 1969.

Rogers, Carl. *Courses by Newspaper.*

Rousseau, J.J.. *Du Contrat Social.* Bartlett's Familiar Quotations, Boston: Little, Brown and Company, 1968.

Rousseau, J.J. *Emile.* Bartlett's Familiar Quotations. Boston: Little, Brown and Company, 1968.

Royster, Vermont. *Orient Express.* Wall Street Journal, February 12, 1980.

San Jose Mercury, November 6, 1980.

San Mateo Times, October 16, 1980.

Sauzey, Francois. *Henry Kissinger,* Trialogue No.19 (Fall 1978).

Shepardson, Whitney H.. *Early History of the Council on Foreign Relations.* Stamford: Overbrook Press, 1960.

Sutton, Antony C.. *Western Technology and Soviet Economic Development 1917 to 1930*. Stanford: Hoover Institution Publications, 1968.

Sutton, Antony C.. *Western Technology and Soviet Economic Development 1930 to 1945*. Stanford: Hoover Institution Publications, 1971.

Sutton, Antony C.. *Wall Street and the Rise of Hitler*. California: '76 Press, 1976.

Sutton, Antony C., *Influence of the Trilateral Commission — Part I,* Trilateral Observer, Volume 2 Number 3 (March 1979). Subscription $60.00 per year from Trilateral Observer, P.O. Box 582, Scottsdale, Arizona 85252.

Ulrich, Roger. *Control of Human Behavior*. Glenview, Illinois: Scott Foresman, 1966.

Villamarest, Pierre de. *La Trilaterale, le C.F.R.* Permanances Numero, April 1978.

Villamarest, Pierre de. *La Lettre d'Information*. Subscription 400 French francs per year from C.E.I. La Vendomiere, 27930 Le Cierrey, France.

Villamarest, Pierre de. *La Trilaterale,* Permanances Numero, April 1978.

Walt, General Lewis W. *The Eleventh Hour*. New York: Caroline House, 1979.

McBernie, W.S. *The Trilateral Commission: Americas New Secret Government*. California: Community Churches of America.

Washington Post, December 24, 1978, p. D4.

Wise, Jennings C.. *Woodrow Wilson: Disciple of Revolution*. New York: Paisley Press, 1938.

INDEX

INDEX

CLIP AND MAIL THIS COUPON TO ENTER YOUR SUBSCRIPTION!

Please enter my subscription as follows:

- ☐ *One year — $75.00*
- ☐ *Six Months — $43.00*

☐ *Enclosed is my check for: $* _____

☐ *Please charge my Visa/Mastercharge for*

$ _____ *Exp.* _____

Card Number _____

_____
Your Signature

* *For overseas subscriptions, add 25%.*

Name _____

Address _____

_____
City _____ State _____ Zip Code

The T.O. is the only intelligence service in the world that spends full time studying and writing about the **Commission**. T.O. is written by eminently qualified Antony Sutton, author of many best selling books, including *Trilaterals Over Washington* and *The War on Gold*.

Will you allow yourself to be kept in the dark any longer? Your subscription will include a special three ring binder with an index to catalogue your issues. Your current issue will reach you about the first of every month.

If for any reason you don't agree that T.O. is *THE* source of documentation on the goals and activities of the **Trilateral Commission**, simply return all items originally sent you within 15 days of receipt and your money will be refunded. **YOU RISK NOTHING!**

ORDER ADDITIONAL COPIES OF
TRILATERALS OVER WASHINGTON

Gentlemen:

Please send . . .

☐ _____ sets of Trilateral Over
Washington at $12.95 each postpaid
(Give one to a friend!)

☐ A one year subscription to the
Trilateral Observer, $75.00

☐ Enclosed is my check for $ _____

Charge to my ☐ Master Charge   ☐ VISA

(Exp. date) _____

Acct. # _____

X_____
   signature

_____
name

_____
street   apt.

_____
city

_____
state   zip

August
CORPORATION
Post Office Box 582   Scottsdale, Arizona 85252

ORDER ADDITIONAL COPIES OF
TRILATERALS OVER WASHINGTON

Gentlemen:

Please send . . .

☐ _____ sets of Trilateral Over
Washington at $12.95 each postpaid
(Give one to a friend!)

☐ A one year subscription to the
Trilateral Observer, $75.00

☐ Enclosed is my check for $ _____

Charge to my ☐ Master Charge   ☐ VISA

(Exp. date) _____

Acct. # _____

X_____
signature

_____
name

_____
street   apt.

_____
city

_____
state   zip

August
CORPORATION
Post Office Box 582   Scottsdale, Arizona 85252